BASIC / NOT BORING
MATH SKILLS

PROBLEM
SOLVING

Grades 6–8⁺

Inventive Exercises to Sharpen
Skills and Raise Achievement

Series Concept & Development
by Imogene Forte & Marjorie Frank
Exercises by Marjorie Frank

Incentive Publications, Inc.
Nashville, Tennessee

Our special thanks to
William Bridges,
our eighth-grade consultant

About the cover:
Bound resist, or tie dye, is the most ancient known method
of fabric surface design. The brilliance of the basic tie dye
design on this cover reflects the possibilities that emerge
from the mastery of basic skills.

Illustrated by Kathleen Bullock
Cover art by Mary Patricia Deprez, dba Tye Dye Mary®
Cover design by Marta Drayton, Joe Shibley, and W. Paul Nance
Edited by Anna Quinn

ISBN 978-0-86530-368-3

8   9   10   11   10   09

PRINTED IN THE UNITED STATES OF AMERICA
www.incentivepublications.com

TABLE OF CONTENTS

CELEBRATE BASIC MATH SKILLS

Basic does not mean boring! There certainly is nothing dull about tracking down solutions to sticky situations and finding out . . .

    . . . how far the coach has to walk when the team bus runs out of gas

    . . . which skier will win the most gold medals

    . . . how deep in debt scuba diver Scott gets buying new equipment

    . . . the number of bones in the feet of a weight-lifting team

    . . . whether Kate Kayaker survives a run through Last Chance Gorge

    . . . how many pizzas the cross-country team can eat after a meet

    . . . the number of falls taken by water-skiers and ice-skaters

The idea of celebrating the basics is just what it sounds like—enjoying and improving the basic skills of solving math problems. The pages that follow are full of exercises for students that will help to review and strengthen specific, basic skills in the content area of math. This is not just another ordinary "fill-in-the-blanks" way to learn. The high-interest activities will put students to work applying a rich variety of the most important skills while enjoying fun and challenging adventures with numbers, ideas, and sports-related dilemmas.

The pages in this book can be used in many ways:

    • for individual students to sharpen a particular skill

    • with a small group needing to relearn or strengthen a skill

    • as an instructional tool for teaching a skill to any size group

    • by students working on their own

    • by students working under the direction of an adult

Each page may be used to introduce a new skill, reinforce a skill, or assess a student's ability to perform a skill.

As students take on the challenges of these adventures with problems, they will grow in their mastery of basic skills and will have a good time while they're doing it. And as you watch them check off the basic problem-solving skills they've strengthened, you can celebrate with them!

SKILLS CHECKLIST FOR PROBLEM SOLVING

✔	SKILL	PAGE(S)
	Identify and define a problem	10, 11
	Eliminate excess information	10, 11, 13
	Identify information needed for problem solution	10–13
	Solve problems using information from illustrations	14
	Select appropriate operation(s) for solving problems	15, 16, 26, 33–37, 43, 44
	Solve problems using information from charts and tables	15–17, 21
	Solve multi-step problems	15–20, 26, 33–48
	Solve problems using information from graphs	18, 19
	Use estimation to solve problems	19, 24
	Solve problems using information from maps	20
	Solve problems using statistical data	21
	Choose and use formulas to solve problems	22
	Use mental math to solve problems	23, 24
	Choose correct equations to solve problems	25, 26
	Translate problems into equations	26
	Use trial and error to solve problems	27
	Create diagrams, charts, or graphs to solve problems	28–31
	Use logic to solve problems	29, 30, 43, 44
	Solve problems involving ratio	32, 38–41
	Solve problems involving proportion	32, 41
	Solve problems involving percent	32–36
	Solve consumer problems	33–37
	Solve problems involving rate, time, and distance	39, 40
	Solve problems involving time and time zones	42
	Solve open-ended problems	43, 44
	Choose appropriate problem-solving strategies	43–46
	Use alternative problem-solving strategies	43–46
	Check accuracy of solutions	47
	Determine reasonableness of solutions	48

PROBLEM SOLVING

Skills Exercises

2-4-6-8!

WHAT DO WE

APPRECIATE?

MATH!

RIGHT ON TRACK

To solve a math problem, you need to be able to identify what information in the problem is needed for finding a solution. For each problem below, circle the letters of the pieces of information that are needed in order to find the solution. Then solve the problem. Use a separate piece of paper for your work.

1. a. Maria won 4 out of her last 7 races.
    b. Her best time is 12 minutes 14 seconds.
    c. She runs the 100 meter race.

Problem: At this rate, how many races will she win out of the next 35?

Answer: _____

2. a. Cy's pole has broken 12 times this year.
    b. It costs $22 to fix a pole every time it is broken.
    c. Cy has used his pole for 39 track meets in the last 2 years.

Problem: How much did Cy pay this year for repairs?

Answer: _____

3. a. Hannah, a hurdler, slept 8 hours 30 minutes on Monday night.
    b. She slept 7 hours on both Tuesday night and Friday night.
    c. She slept 6 hours 20 minutes on Wednesday night.
    d. She got up at 6:30 A.M. on Thursday.

Problem: How much sleep did she get in the 3 nights before Thursday's meet?

Answer: _____

4. a. The track meet started at 4:00 P.M. on Monday.
    b. The high jump bar was knocked off 16 times.
    c. Justin has placed first 13 times in this event.
    d. There were a total of 52 jumps.

Problem: What is the ratio of unsuccessful jumps to total jumps (in lowest terms)?

Answer: _____

Name _____

10

RIGHT ON TRACK, CONTINUED

5. a. Abby washes her uniform after every meet.
    b. There are 3 meets a week.
    c. It shrinks .8% every time she washes it.
Problem: In what week of the season will the uniform have shrunk 12%?

Answer: _____

6. a. The decathlon lasts 2 days, with 5 events each day.
    b. Dylan eats 4000 calories each day for 7 days before the event.
    c. Dylan eats nothing for the 2 days of the event.
Problem: What is the average number of calories consumed per day for the 9 days?

Answer: _____

7. a. There were 900 spectators at the track meet on Friday.
    b. The crowd on Saturday was 3.5 times the size of Friday's.
    c. The crowd on Friday was 1.5 times the size of Sunday's crowd.
Problem: How many fans were there on Sunday?

Answer: _____

8. a. The male track and field athletes drank 153 gallons of sports drink at the meet.
    b. The track and field athletes drank 255 gallons of sports drink.
    c. The women track and field athletes drank 102 gallons.
Problem: What percent of the sports drink was drunk by the women?

Answer: _____

9. a. Paul's shot put weighs 16 pounds.
    b. Paul weighs 190 pounds.
    c. His record distance is 1.3 meters longer than Ray's.
    d. His record is .7 meters shorter than Gregorio's.
    e. Gregorio's record is 17.1 meters.
Problem: What is Paul's record distance for the shot put?

Answer: _____

10. a. The track and field area is 900 x 500 feet, including track and stands.
    b. The grass is mowed twice a week.
    c. 5200 square feet of the sports area is not grass.
Problem: How many square feet of grass are mowed each week?

Answer: _____

Name

11

SOMETHING'S MISSING

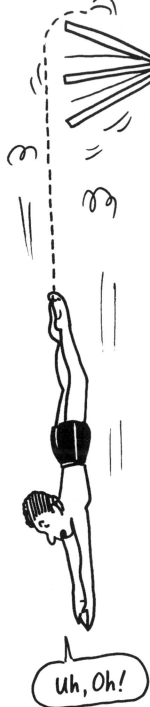

Some information is missing in these problems. For each one, tell what other information you would need in order to solve the problem.

1. This daring diver holds the record for gold medals in his state. How many more medals does he have than his nearest competitor?

   Missing: _____

2. The diving board is 12 feet above the water's surface. When David springs up, he rises 3 feet. What is the total number of feet he travels up and down from the time he leaves the board until his fingertips touch the bottom of the pool?

   Missing: _____

3. Deanna can compete with 8 different dives. She practices each of these several times a day. How many practice dives does she do in 7 days?

   Missing: _____

4. The Benson High Swimming and Diving Team used 48 towels at Tuesday's practice. What percent of the pile of towels was left unused?

   Missing: _____

5. The world record high dive is 176 feet 10 inches. What is the difference between Maria's highest dive and the world record?

   Missing: _____

6. 5 out of 7 judges each awarded Jake an 8.5 score on his high board dive. His total was 60.5 points. What score did the seventh judge give him?

   Missing: _____

7. The diving pool at Amanda's school is 48 feet wide and 84 feet long. What is the capacity of the pool?

   Missing: _____

8. Greg Louganis holds 17 U.S. national diving titles. How many of these did he win before the 1984 Olympics?

   Missing: _____

9. Randy's scores on all his springboard dives this year total 722.5 points. How does this total compare to the average for the team?

   Missing: _____

POOL DRAINED
FOR CLEANING

uh, Oh!

Name

12

HOW MUCH IS TOO MUCH?

Sometimes there is too much information in math problems. Then you have to decide what is really necessary. For each of these problems, underline the information that is NOT needed for a solution. Then find the answer and write it on the line.

1. Lana, a long distance runner, ran 16 miles in 3½ hours. She left home at 11 A.M. and returned at 2:30 P.M. At the end of the run her pulse was 145 beats per minute. What is the rate of her speed in miles per hour?

    Answer _____

2. Nicole left home at 9:18 A.M. to jog with 2 friends. She ran 2.6 miles to Sam's house, and then she and Sam ran 4.1 miles to meet Rog. Rog ran with them 1.7 more miles. How many miles did Sam run?

    Answer _____

3. After a cross-country race, Juan's team ate 12 pizzas. 6 were vegetarian, 4 were plain cheese, and 2 had pepperoni. There were 18 runners on the team. On the average, what fraction of a pizza did each runner eat?

    Answer _____

4. Annika's best time for a 10 k race is 55 minutes. Yesterday she left home at 3:16 P.M. and returned at 4:20 P.M. She ran approximately .16 k per minute. How much time did her run take?

    Answer _____

5. 500 runners took part in a 15 k run. 212 were male. 1.4% of the runners did not finish. 4 males did not finish. The winner was 36 years old. The average age of the runners was 28. How many women finished the race?

    Answer _____

6. James wears out 4 pairs of running shoes each year. They cost him about $70 a pair. He spent $60 this year for entrance fees in races. Approximately how much does he spend on his shoes in 3 years?

    Answer _____

7. Jessica traveled 830 miles by car to 12 cross-country meets this year. At these races she ran a total of 111 miles. She spent $490 on traveling expenses. How many fewer miles did she run than she traveled in the car?

    Answer _____

8. Each member of the 36-member cross-country team has 3 different 2-piece uniforms. These uniforms cost $55 each. When they wash all their uniforms at the Laundromat on a trip, how many pieces of clothing get washed?

    Answer _____

Name _____

SHAPE-UPS

Use the illustration to find the solutions to the following problems.

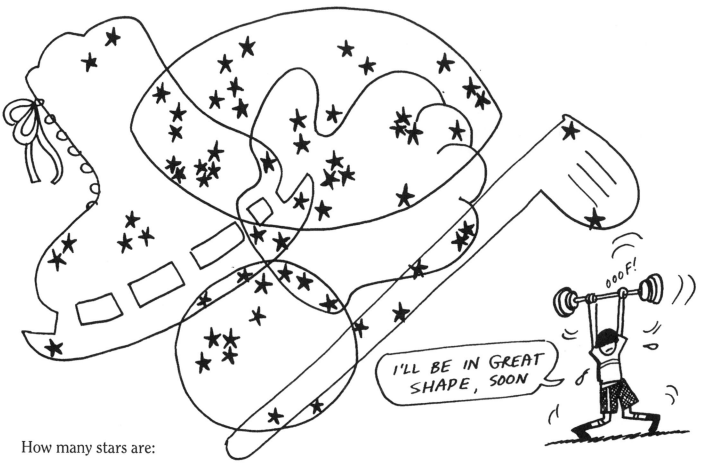

I'LL BE IN GREAT SHAPE, SOON

OOOF!

How many stars are:

1. in the intersection of the football and the baseball?

2. not in the skate?

3. in the football but not in the mitt?

4. in the golf club but outside any other shape?

5. in the intersection of the baseball and golf club?

6. in the intersection of the skate, football, and mitt?

7. in the football but outside the skate?

8. total in the mitt and in the golf club?

9. in the intersection of the baseball and skate?

10. in the mitt and in no other shape?

11. not in the glove or the football?

12. not in any shape?

13. in the skate but not in the mitt or football?

14. in the baseball but in no other shape?

15. inside only one shape?

16. total in the mitt plus total in the skate?

17. in the intersection of the football, golf club, and mitt?

18. in the intersection of the mitt, baseball, and golf club?

Name

FARE WARS

These players are making ticket choices for their island vacations. For each question below, tell what mathematical **operation** or **operations** the player would use to solve his or her problem. Then solve the problem. Use a separate piece of paper for your work.

Destination	Paradise Air	Tropic Jet	SunFun Jet
JAMAICA	Child $255 Adult $325	All Seats $295	All Seats $300
FIJI	Child $470 Adult $640	Child $400 Adult $690	Child $295 Adult $770
BERMUDA	All Seats $410	1st Class $800 Tourist $400	Child $399 Adult $420
HAWAII	All Seats $525	$600 3rd person flies free	Child $400 Adult $535
TAHITI	All Seats $700	All Seats $690	Child $600 Adult $750

HOLD THE PLANE! I CAN'T FIND THE COACH!

I NEED A SEAT BY THE RESTROOM, M'AM.

CAN I PAY ON THE INSTALLMENT PLAN?

1. What will Tim pay for 4 adults to Hawaii on Tropic Jet?

   Operation(s) _____ Answer _____

2. Tad wants to take 2 adults and 1 child to Jamaica. Which airline is the best deal? What will Tad pay?

   Operation(s) _____ Answer _____

3. How much will Ted save by flying to Tahiti on Tropic Jet instead of Paradise Air? He is traveling with his older brother and his two kids.

   Operation(s) _____ Answer _____

4. Tom wants to take 4 friends to Bermuda first class. Can he do this for $2000?

   Operation(s) _____ Answer _____

5. What is the cheapest tropical vacation Todd can arrange for himself, his wife, and 3 kids? On what airline?

   Operation(s) _____ Answer _____

6. Is it cheaper to fly 4 adults and 3 children to Fiji on SunFun Jet, to Bermuda on Tropic Jet, or to Hawaii on Paradise Air?

   Operation(s) _____ Answer _____

Name _____

ATHLETES ON THE LINE

The athletes at a California summer sports camp make a lot of phone calls. Use the information from the chart on the next page (p. 17) to answer the questions about costs of their calls. Use separate paper for your work.

1. Gymnast Joe called home to Moscow, Idaho, at 9 P.M. on Thursday. The call was 14 minutes long. How much did it cost? _____

2. Biker Becky made a 20-minute call home to Pearl City, Hawaii, that cost $24.70. When did she call? _____

3. Kayaker Suzie talked 14 minutes to her boyfriend in Paris, South Carolina, on Saturday at 9 A.M. How much did it cost? _____

4. Climber Claudia, from Romeo, Colorado, called home on Friday at 11 P.M. and talked 7 minutes. After that she called Moody, Alabama, for 5 minutes. How much did her calls cost? _____

5. Pitcher Paula talked to her sister in Sassafras, Kentucky, for 1 hour on July 4th. How much did her call cost? Was this more or less than she spent calling her friend in Sugar Hill, Georgia, the next day, Friday, at 1 P.M. for 30 minutes?

_____

6. Sprinter Shawn talked to his coach in Nutley, New Jersey, on Wednesday at 7 P.M. The call cost $12.24. How long did he talk? _____

7. Did Dan the diver spend more money talking 6 minutes to his parents in Onset, Massachusetts, at noon on Wednesday or 25 minutes to his girlfriend in Talent, Oregon, on Thursday at 9:30 P.M? _____

8. Equestrian Eddie made three calls to friends between 10 and 11:30 P.M. on Saturday: 5 minutes to Hoxie, Kansas, 19 minutes to King Salmon, Alaska, and 12 minutes to Suncook, Nevada. How much did he spend on the calls? _____

9. Golfer Gina had only $12.30 to spend on phone calls. How long could she talk to her friend in Claypool, Arizona, after 11 P.M. on Tuesday? _____

10. How long was wrestler Ramon's $10.50 call home to Story, WY on Tuesday at 11:00 A.M?

_____

Name _____

Use this chart to solve the problems on page 16.

CITY CALLED	WEEK DAYS, Monday–Friday						SAT, SUN, & HOLIDAYS	
	8 A.M.–5 P.M.		5 P.M.–11 P.M.		11 P.M.–8 A.M.		All Hours	
	First 3 min.	Add. min.	First 3 min.	Add. min.	First 3 min.	Add. min.	First 3 min.	Add. min.
Moody, Alabama	3.60	.96	2.80	.78	1.95	.58	2.00	.62
King Salmon, Alaska	2.90	.75	2.40	.60	1.50	.43	1.80	.58
Claypool, Arizona	1.98	.50	1.66	.38	1.10	.28	1.26	.30
Romeo, Colorado	2.10	.54	1.75	.42	1.30	.28	1.62	.35
Sugar Hill, Georgia	3.15	.78	2.72	.66	1.75	.36	1.88	.45
Pearl City, Hawaii	4.30	1.20	3.96	.98	2.50	.68	2.65	.75
Moscow, Idaho	2.00	.60	1.62	.50	1.20	.35	1.46	.40
Hoxie, Kansas	2.60	.70	1.90	.58	1.50	.35	1.76	.44
Sassafras, Kentucky	3.20	1.00	2.90	.90	1.80	.64	2.00	.74
Onset, Massachusetts	3.96	1.04	3.18	.88	2.02	.66	2.32	.70
Paradise, Montana	1.95	.54	1.66	.48	1.00	.38	1.18	.44
Suncook, Nevada	2.05	.65	1.65	.55	1.25	.40	1.35	.50
Nutley, New Jersey	3.34	1.00	2.88	.78	1.86	.65	1.95	.75
Talent, Oregon	1.60	.48	1.05	.38	.90	.30	.98	.36
Pascoag, Rhode Island	3.35	1.14	2.88	.86	1.78	.66	2.00	.75
Paris, South Carolina	3.44	1.05	2.96	.95	1.85	.70	2.10	.80
Camelot, Texas	3.00	.86	2.25	.70	1.65	.50	1.75	.56
Story, Wyoming	2.22	.46	1.86	.38	1.30	.25	1.40	.30

Name

GO FOR THE GOLD

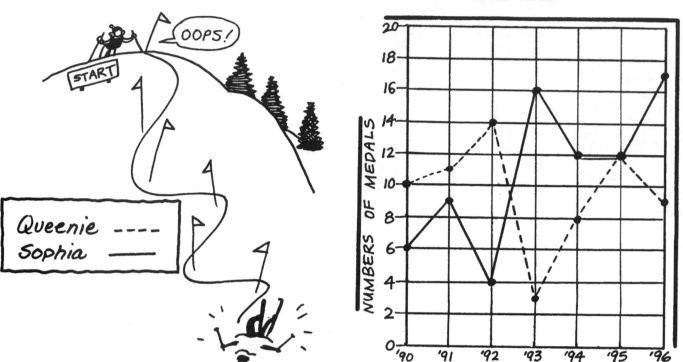

Queenie - - - -
Sophia ———

Queenie Quick-Turn and Sophia Schusher have been fierce slalom rivals for years. They are the top two women on the world circuit. The graph shows their gold medal totals for the past 7 years. Use the graph to answer the questions below.

1. As of 1992, who had the most medals (total)? _____

2. How many more did Sophia win in her best year than in her worst? _____

3. Who had the largest drop from 1 year to the next? _____

4. Who had the greatest gain from 1 year to the next?_____

5. Who had the greatest gain in a 2-year period? _____

6. What year did they tie in number of medals? _____

7. In what 3-year period did Queenie win more than Sophia?_____

8. Who had the best record from 93 to 95?_____

9. This equation shows Queenie's wins in comparison to Sophia's for what year? _____

$$Q = 3S + 2$$

10. Who won the most gold medals in the 7-year period?_____

11. In 1993, Sophia won twice as many medals as Queenie did in what year? _____

12. Who had the best record from 90-95?_____

Name

18

RECORD ATTENDANCE

Use the bar graph to answer these questions about attendance at sporting events.
Estimate the answers.

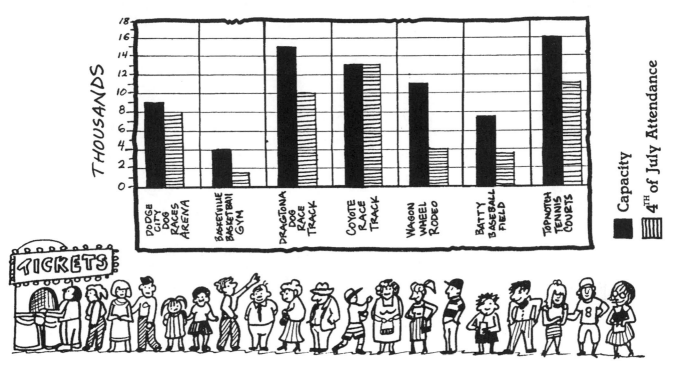

1. Which 2 centers had about the same attendance on July 4th?

   _____

   _____

2. What is the difference between the capacity of the Dodge City Dog Race Arena and the attendance on July 4th?

   _____

3. Which arena has a difference of about 2500 between its capacity and the July 4th attendance?

   _____

4. What is the difference between the capacity of the largest and the smallest arenas?

   _____

5. How many more people attended the Dragtona Dog Race on July 4th than attended the Batty baseball game?

   _____

6. How many fewer people watched the Wagonwheel Rodeo cowboys than the Topnotch tennis players?

   _____

7. Which 2 centers had a difference of about 5000 between capacity and July 4th attendance?

   _____

8. How many fewer people watched the basketball game than the Coyote races on July 4th?

   _____

Name _____

ON THE ROAD AGAIN

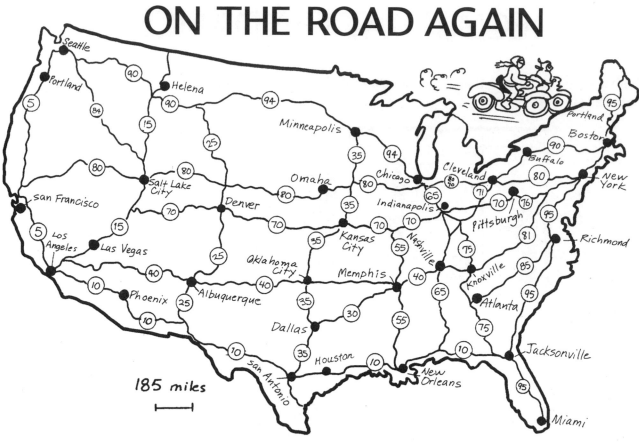

185 miles

Nora and Nancy, the Dare Devil Racing Duo, are traveling to races around the country. Use the map to help you answer questions about their travels.

1. If they ride 1480 miles west on I-80 from Chicago, where do they end up?

   _____

2. Next stop: from Portland south on I-5 to San Francisco. About how far will they travel?

   _____

3. For their toughest race, they head east from Salt Lake City, Nevada, on I-80, then south on I-35 to Oklahoma City. Approximately how long is their trip in miles?

   _____

4. From Memphis, Tennessee, they head for New York City. Tell the shortest route and the approximate mileage.

   _____

5. If they ride about 500-600 miles from Albuquerque, what cities could they reach?

   _____

6. What is the approximate mileage of this route: from Indianapolis south on I-65 to Nashville, I-40 west to Memphis, I-30 west to Dallas, and I-35 south to San Antonio?

   _____

7. They ride about 1500 miles north from Miami on I-95. Where do they end up?

   _____

8. Their last race takes them from Helena to Oklahoma City by routes I-15, I-90, I-94, and I-35. Is this the shortest route? If not, what is the shortest route?

   _____

Name

SOCCER STATISTICS

Use the statistics on the charts below to solve the problems about the performances of Suzannah, the year's highest scoring striker, and Gregory, the school's best goalie.

SUZANNAH STRIKER		
GAME	ATTEMPTS	GOALS
1	8	2
2	4	0
3	9	2
4	11	3
5	12	3
6	5	1
7	7	2
8	13	4
9	5	1
10	8	1

SUZANNAH

1. Total goals she scored in 10 games _____

2. Her total attempts in the year _____

3. The ratio of goals to attempts _____

4. The percent of success in game 8 _____

5. Best game for ratio of goals to attempts _____

6. The games that had the greatest difference between attempts and goals scored _____

7. Number of unsuccessful attempts _____

8. Worst stretch of 3 games for ratio of scores to attempts _____

GREGORY GOALIE		
GAME	ATTEMPTS ON GOAL	GOALS SCORED
1	8	0
2	12	1
3	9	2
4	18	3
5	16	0
6	7	1
7	10	0
8	15	2
9	11	1
10	20	4

GREGORY

9. Total goals scored against him _____

10. Total goals he stopped _____

11. Ratio of goals scored to goals attempted against him _____

12. Total goals he stopped in games 5-10 _____

13. Percent of goals stopped during 10 games _____

14. Difference between goals attempted and goals scored in game 10 _____

15. Best 3 games for ratio of stops to attempts _____

16. Worst game for ratio of stops to attempts _____

Name _____

THE RIGHT FORMULA

Use the formulas below to answer these questions. Round your answers to the nearest tenth. You may need to work the problems on an extra sheet of paper.

Area of triangle .... $A = \frac{1}{2}bh$
Area of square .... $A = s^2$
Area of rectangle .... $A = l \times w$
Area of trapezoid .... $A = \frac{1}{2}h\,(b_1 + b_2)$
Area of circle .... $A = \pi r^2$

Perimeter of triangle ...... $P = a + b + c$
Perimeter of square .... $P = 4s$
Perimeter of rectangle .... $P = s(l + w)$
Circumference of circle .. $C = 2\pi r$

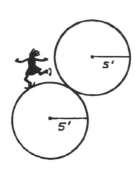

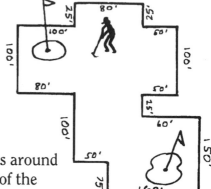

1. A figure skater goes around her figure 8 three times during a test. How much distance does she cover? _____

2. A horse trots around the outside of the golf course. How far does she trot?

_____

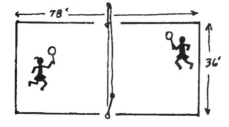

3. How much area is on either side of the net on the tennis court? _____

4. Jan's coach paces around the tennis court 5 times before the match begins. How far does the coach walk? _____

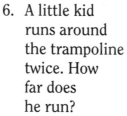

6. A little kid runs around the trampoline twice. How far does he run?

_____

5. How much area is there for the boxers to dance around in?

7. What area is available for the trampolinist to land on?

_____

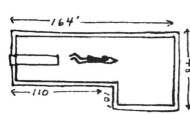

8. If you had to paint the bottom of the pool, how much area would you cover? _____

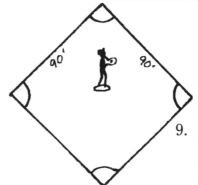

9. How far does a batter run to complete a home run?

10. It's Nyoko's job to clean the sail on her mom's boat. After she scrubs the front and back of the sail, how much surface area has she cleaned?

Name _____

MENTAL PUSH-UPS

Try to solve each of these problems in your head. Write your answer on the line.

1. Jay does 90 sit-ups in 2 minutes. At this rate, how many can he do in 10 minutes? _____

2. Lu does 18 push-ups, 166 sit-ups, 37 jumping jacks, and 11 chin-ups. How many repetitions of exercises has she completed? _____

3. Chad grunts 3 times as often as Jeff when he's doing pull-ups. Jeff grunts 11 times a minute. How many times does Chad grunt in 5 minutes? _____

4. Jennifer walks the treadmill slowly for 8 minutes and fast for another 68 minutes. What fraction of the total time is she going slowly (in lowest terms)? _____

5. Tomas begins his workout at 1:35 P.M. and finishes at 3:01 P.M. How long does he work out? _____

6. Jo's pulse climbs 115 beats per minute to 190 bpm while he is jumping rope. What was his heart rate when he started?_____

7. Jess exercised 40 minutes every day this week except for 55 minutes on Tuesday and Friday. What is her total exercise time this week? _____

8. Bryan's dad gave him 5 cents for every sit-up and 50 cents for each push-up he could do. He did 130 sit-ups and 35 push-ups. How much money did he receive? _____

9. Drinking water costs 85 cents at the gym. How many bottles can Moe buy for $10?_____

10. Melanie has 8 different exercise outfits. She wears a different one each day and doesn't wear it again until she's worn all the others. How many times will she wear outfit # 1 in the month of December if she wears it on December 1st and exercises each day? _____

11. The exercise mat is 13 meters long and 9 meters wide. Lulu jogs around it once. How far around is it?_____

12. Jan does 80 back stretches today. Mandy does ⅖ as many. How many is that? _____

13. Jenna's workout this Monday is on June 25. What day is her August 10 workout? _____

14. Joe talks to a friend 3 minutes after every 7 minutes he exercises at the gym. After 1 hour at the gym, how many minutes has Joe exercised? _____

Name _____

23

SWIMMER'S SNACK BREAK

Tacos ----- # .80
Burritos ----- .99
Hot Dogs ----- 1.50
Hamburgers -- 1.75
Pizza Slice -- 1.25
Sandwiches -- 1.90
Rice Bowl -- 1.00
Fries ----- .95
Salad ----- 1.10
Chips ----- .50
Shakes ----- 1.50
Drinks ----- .90
Ice Cream ---- .95
Candy ----- .45

The championship Surfside Swim Team is taking some time out from their strenuous practice for a snack break. Estimate each swimmer's total bill. Write your estimate on the ticket.

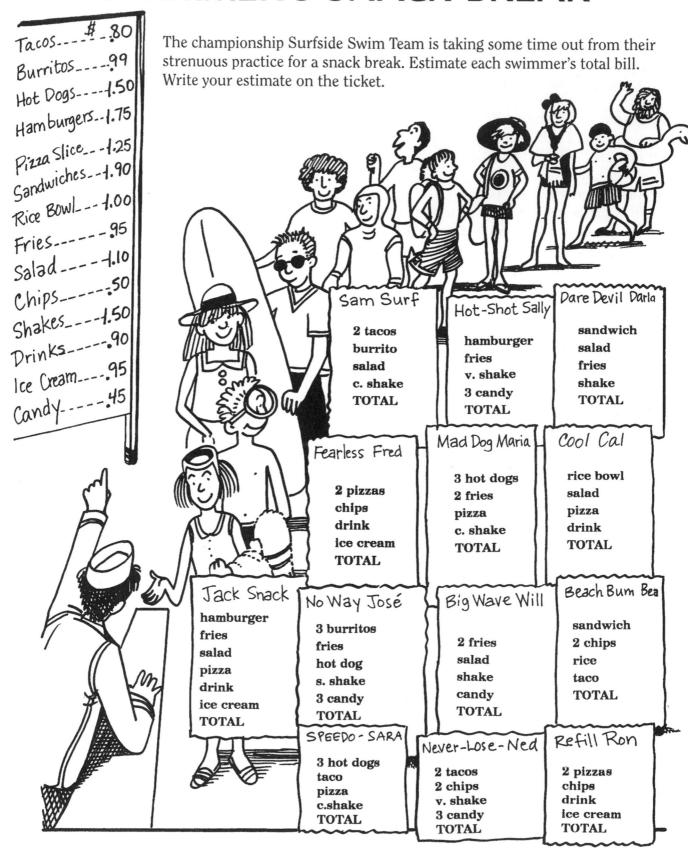

Sam Surf

2 tacos
burrito
salad
c. shake
TOTAL

Hot-Shot Sally

hamburger
fries
v. shake
3 candy
TOTAL

Dare Devil Darla

sandwich
salad
fries
shake
TOTAL

Fearless Fred

2 pizzas
chips
drink
ice cream
TOTAL

Mad Dog Maria

3 hot dogs
2 fries
pizza
c. shake
TOTAL

Cool Cal

rice bowl
salad
pizza
drink
TOTAL

Jack Snack

hamburger
fries
salad
pizza
drink
ice cream
TOTAL

No Way José

3 burritos
fries
hot dog
s. shake
3 candy
TOTAL

Big Wave Will

2 fries
salad
shake
candy
TOTAL

Beach Bum Bea

sandwich
2 chips
rice
taco
TOTAL

SPEEDO - SARA

3 hot dogs
taco
pizza
c.shake
TOTAL

Never-Lose-Ned

2 tacos
2 chips
v. shake
3 candy
TOTAL

Refill Ron

2 pizzas
chips
drink
ice cream
TOTAL

Name

24

A CAREFUL BALANCE

Often you can solve a word problem by turning it into an equation. For each of these, write the letter equation that correctly fits the problem. Then solve the problem.

1. Tatiana falls from the balance beam 3 times during her first 8 routines. At this rate, how many times will she do her routine to end up with 27 falls?
   a) $3/8 = 27/x$
   b) $27/x = 8/3$
   c) $3/27 = x/8$

   Correct Equation _____

   Solution _____

2. 5 days a week Tatiana spends 8 hours at the gym with a $2\frac{1}{4}$-hour break in the late afternoon. On the fourth day, she also takes a $1\frac{1}{2}$-hour morning break. How much time does she spend in actual training at the gym?
   a) $5(8 - 2\frac{1}{4}) + 1\frac{1}{2} = n$
   b) $n = 5(8 - 2\frac{1}{4} - 1\frac{1}{2})$
   c) $n = 5(8 - 2\frac{1}{4}) - 1\frac{1}{2}$
   d) $8 - 2\frac{1}{4} + 1\frac{1}{2} = 5n$

   Correct Equation _____

   Solution _____

3. 26 gymnasts started for the team at the beginning of the year. 2 dropped each week for 8 weeks. Then 3 joined. The final total was equal to 5 less than the number of members on last year's team. How many were on last year's team?
   a) $26 - 2 + 8 - 5 = x$
   b) $26 - (8 \times 2) + 3 = x - 5$
   c) $x = 26 + 5 - 2(8 + 3)$

   Correct Equation _____

   Solution _____

4. Kate's floor routine lasts 0.6 minute less than Meg's and 0.3 longer than Brie's. Brie's routine is 2.4 minutes long. How long does Meg's last?
   a) $2.4 - 0.6 + 0.3 = M$
   b) $M = 2.4 + 0.3 + 0.6$
   c) $2.4 - 0.3 - 0.6 = M$

   Correct Equation _____

   Solution _____

5. Sandra won 9 gold medals in 1993, 14 in 1994, and 8 in 1995. Her total gold medals in these 3 years was twice what she won in 1996. How many in 1996?
   a) $2n = 9 + 14 + 8$
   b) $3(9 - 14 + 8) = n$
   c) $n = 2(9 - 14 + 8)$

   Correct Equation _____

   Solution _____

6. Todd had 8 injuries last year. He had 2 less than 3 times that many this year. How many injuries this year?
   a) $n = 3(8 - 2)$
   b) $n = (3 \times 8) - 2$
   c) $n = 8 - (3 \times 2)$

   Correct Equation _____

   Solution _____

Name _____

FAN-TASTICS

Translate each problem into an equation. Write your equation. Then use the equation to find the solution.

1. The Grizzly football fans are a loyal crowd. In the 1994 season their attendance rose 880 over the '93 season. In '95 it was 1000 more than in '94, setting a season record of 17,964. What was the attendance in '93?

2. When Grandpa Cheer took over leadership of the Grizzly Booster Club, there were 44 members. Now there are 8 less than 3 times that many. How many members now?

3. The principal's twins found 26 wallets under the bleachers. This was 6 less than 4 times the number of wallets the coach's triplets found. How many did the coach's kids find?

4. The Grizzly cheerleaders cheered 12 less than 42 dozen cheers. How many cheers?

5. The Sitalot family came to the game with $12. They bought 4 bags of popcorn at 75¢ each and 3 drinks at $1 each in the first half. At halftime, Sammy Sitalot found 6 quarters under the bleachers. The family went home with $3.45. How much did they spend in the second half?

6. Little Frannie Francis bought a bag of popcorn with 1087 pieces of popcorn in it. She spilled 12 pieces for every 1 she put in her mouth. At the end of the game, there were 34 pieces left. How many pieces actually went into her mouth?

Name _____

26

ON A ROLL

The trial and error method is one strategy for problem solving. First, you choose a solution you think might work and try it out. If it doesn't fit the problem, keep trying others until you find one that works.

Eric is pretty good on his skates, but he's doing such wild stuff that he takes plenty of falls. Find the number that tells how many falls Eric took each day.

DAY 1
An even, 2-digit number whose 2 digits have a difference of 1 and the first digit is larger than the second. The sum of the digits and the product are < 10 and > 0.

DAY 2
The smallest even number other than 2 that is a factor of 78.

DAY 3
A prime number < 10 with a square that is > 40 but < 80.

DAY 4
A 2-digit multiple of 3 whose digits total 6, but neither digit is 1, 2, or 0.

DAY 5
The smallest prime number with more than 1 digit, the sum of whose digits is > 5.

DAY 6
A 2-digit square whose digits add up to an even number.

DAY 7
A number < 50 that is divisible by 1, 2, 3, 5, and 10.

DAY 8
The smallest number divisible by 9.

DAY 9
A number that when added to 52 gives a square number, when subtracted from 48 gives another square, and when divided by 3 gives another square.

DAY 10
A number > 95 and < 115 that is the product of 2 prime numbers (other than 1).

Name

CROSS-COUNTRY CHALLENGE

One strategy for problem solving is to make a chart with the information you're given. For some problems, this is the easiest way to find a solution. For each of these problems below, make a chart to help you find the answer. Show your chart on a separate piece of paper.

1. On the first day Margot skied the Camelback Cross-Country Course, she did it in 26 minutes. Each day after that, she cut 10 seconds off her time. Skier Holly did the same course in 23 minutes on Day 1, cutting 5 seconds off her time each day after that. On what day will the two skiers have the same time on this course?

   Answer _____

2. Michael wants to buy 2 items of food for each of the friends skiing with him. The snack shop has 5 kinds of snacks: granola bars, energy bars, chocolate bars, peanuts, and bananas. How many different combinations of 2 items could he possibly choose?

   Answer _____

3. Four skiers, Ted, Jed, Ned, and Fred, want to practice today. Practice sessions are from 8 to 10:40 A.M. only. Skiers must start the course 10 minutes apart and no more than 3 skiers may be on the course at once. Each skier is allowed to stay on the course for only 30 minutes. Can all 4 skiers practice today and finish before 9:40 A.M.?

   Answer _____

4. Katarina skied 2 miles on Day 1. Each day after that, she skied 1.5 miles more than the day before. On what day did she ski over 30 miles?

   Answer _____

Name _____

WHO'S WHO AT THE STADIUM?

You will need to use logical thinking to find a solution for these problems. The clues will help you. For each problem, draw a diagram to show your thinking.

1. Only one of the cheerleaders at Ashland High has brought a pet to the game. The pets that aren't here are a tarantula, a llama, an iguana, and a pig. The cheerleaders' names are Tori, Tom, Tad, Tish, and Tara. Their ages are 14, 15, 16, 17, and 18. Which cheerleader owns the poodle, and how old is she (or he)?

   Tad is 4 years older than Tara.
   Tish hates dogs and Tom hates pigs.
   Tom's mom won't allow a large pet.
   Tara owns the iguana.
   Tad is afraid of arachnids.
   Tori is older than Tom.
   Tara does not own the pig.
   Tori is allergic to dogs.
   Tish is 2 years younger than Tori.
   Tad is 1 year older than the tarantula owner.
   The pig owner is 3 years older than the llama owner.

   Answer _____

2. The players here are Tyler, Craig, Ray, Sean, and Elijah. Their positions are fullback, quarterback, center, guard, and tackle. What is the name and number of the quarterback?

   Elijah is not a tackle.
   Craig is on one end of the line.
   Ray is not # 4 or # 8.
   The guard is # 8.
   Tyler is not the tackle.
   The quarterback is not Ray.
   The center is # 2.

   The fullback is not Tyler.
   The quarterback is between the guard and tackle.
   Craig is next to Ray.
   # 2 is not Ray.
   Elijah is not next to Sean.

   Answer _____

CONFUSION AT THE FINISH LINE

Draw a diagram to help you solve each of these four logic problems. Each person in each race is mentioned.

1. Daryl and Jake are behind Raoul.
   Kai is faster than Guy.
   There are 2 runners ahead of Hank.
   There are 2 runners between Raoul and Jake.
   Guy is faster than Jake but slower than Hank.
   Hank is behind Kai.
   Jake is ahead of Daryl.   Who wins the race?_____

2. Fran and Meghan are ahead of Patrice.
   Fran is behind Anya and ahead of Tonia.
   Carla is the second runner ahead of Fran.
   3 runners are between Tonia and Carla.
   Meghan is ahead of Fran but behind Anya.   Who wins the race?_____

3. Josh is ahead of Wynn, but behind Gabe.
   There are 3 people between Gabe and Bryan.
   Andy is behind Josh.   Who wins the race?_____

4. Tori is behind Tracy
   Trina is ahead of Tracy.
   Trish is ahead of Tori.
   Tori is the 4th runner behind Tami.   Who wins the race? _____

Name

BOUNCE BACK

Draw a diagram or a picture to help you solve each of these problems.

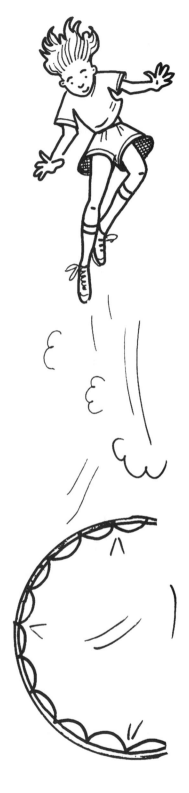

1. As Jamey bounces on the trampoline, 11 coins totaling $1.37 fall out of his pocket.

   What are these coins? _____

2. He keeps bouncing and more coins bounce out of the other pocket. The total this time is $2.10 from 14 coins.

   What are the coins? _____

3. A group of kids are standing evenly spaced around a circular trampoline, watching the tricks of the trampolinist. Kid #11 is directly across from Kid #27.

   How many spectators are there around the trampoline? _____

4. The instructor is trying to divide a group of trampolinists into teams for a competition. If he puts them into groups of 2, 4, or 6, one is left over. If the groups have 7, none are left over.

   How many trampolinists are there? _____

5. Ryan is trying to walk across the length of a trampoline while Jude is bouncing. The trampoline is 27 feet long. Each step Ryan takes moves him forward 2.3 feet, but each time he moves, one of Jude's bounces sends him back .5 foot.

   How many steps will it take him to get across? _____

Name

Basic Skills/Problem Solving 6-8+

CHANCE FOR A BULL'S-EYE

You may not be as sharp as Alonzo with an arrow, but you can probably
help him solve some of these problems about percent and ratio.
Round each problem to the nearest whole number.

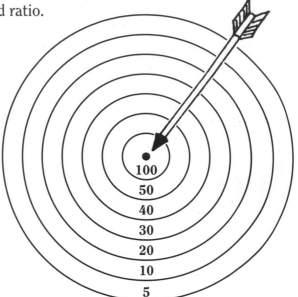

1. If Alonzo got 4 bull's-eyes out of 22 shots,
   what is his percentage of perfect shots? _____

2. He hit the wall 3 times out of 33 shots.
   What percent of all shots is this? _____

3. 40% of Alonzo's 55 shots today
   have been hitting the 50 ring.
   How many shots is this? _____

4. Alonzo's archer friend, Abigail, practices
   7 out of every 10 days. How many days
   has she practiced in the last 10 weeks? _____

5. Today, Abigail has brought 12 sandwiches to share with friends at
   practice. Unfortunately, her pet mouse got into her backpack and ate parts
   of 5 of them. What percent of the sandwiches are still in good shape? _____

6. Alonzo's first practice round score is 165. If he shot 6 arrows, then
   he scored what percent of the total possible points for that round? _____

7. Each arrow costs $3.40, and Alonzo breaks 10% of all the arrows he
   buys. If he buys 150, how much money does he lose on broken arrows? _____

8. Abigail's high school has 2500 students. The girls'
   archery team has .6% of the school's students as
   members. How many members does the team have? _____

9. If Alonzo hits the 100 ring once, the 50 ring twice,
   the 40 three times, the 30 twice, and the 10 twice,
   what percent of the total points are provided by
   the arrows that have hit the 10 and 30 rings? _____

10. If the archery team gets a bull's-eye on 20% of their
    total shots today, and the number of bull's-eyes is 27,
    how many shots did they take all together? _____

Name _____

SPORTS STUFF ON SALE

The Giorgiano family went shopping before Tim, Tom, Tami, Terry, and Troy went off to sports camp. They found a great sale at the Super Duper Sports Center. Find the price they paid at each section of the store.

1. soccer shoes   89.50
   football cleats   63.96
   basketball shoes   89.99

   total   _____

   discount   _____

   sale price   _____

2. tennis shorts   32.00
   tennis shoes   66.85
   duffel bag   24.95
   (can) tennis balls   2.90

   total   _____

   discount   _____

   sale price   _____

3. aquasox   35.50
   swimsuit   30.00
   snorkel   24.85
   wet suit   177.00
   fins   55.00

   total   _____

   discount   _____

   sale price   _____

4. jogging shoes   79.95
   warm-up suit   126.00
   sweatbands   10.00
   stop watch   17.99

   total   _____

   discount   _____

   sale price   _____

5. helmet   34.45
   bike shorts   19.00
   gloves   18.00
   reflectors   2.50

   total   _____

   discount   _____

   sale price   _____

6. What is the total they saved? _____

Name _____

TICKET TIE-UPS

Use the information on the chart to answer each question about discounted prices for these fans who are buying tickets to sports events.

TICKETS

Baseball Game..................	29.00 Adult 18.00 Child
Tennis Match....................	16.00 All Tickets
Gymnastics Events...........	10.00 Semifinals 30.00 Finals
Diving Finals	22.00 Adult 10.00 Child
Fencing Finals..................	36.00 All Tickets
Volleyball Game................	40.00 All Tickets
Golf Tournament..............	36.00 All Tickets
Swim Events.....................	15.00 Adult 12.00 Child
Track Events.....................	19.00 1-Day Pass 35.00 2-Day Pass

1. The Perez family bought tickets for 2 adults and 3 children to the diving finals and the gymnastic finals. They have a coupon for a 15% discount. How much will they pay? _____

2. The Johannes sisters, both children, have a coupon for a 10% discount on the 2-day track events and 20% off the baseball game and the swim events. How much will they pay if they go to all three? _____

TWO FOR TENNIS

3. Mrs. Switchalot gets a 35% discount for senior citizens. She wants to turn in her 2 tickets from the golf tournament and see the volleyball game and the fencing finals with a friend. If she pays for her friend's tickets as well as her own, how much more will she pay? _____

4. The whole Cue family reunion of 16 adults and 22 kids wants to see the diving finals. They qualify for a 40% group discount. How much will they pay? _____

Name _____

TICKET TIE-UPS, CONTINUED

5. Mrs. Shivers qualifies for a 25% discount as a member of the Friends of Spiders and other Arthropods Club. How much will it cost her to buy 4 child and 2 adult tickets to both gymnastics events if she uses her 25% discount coupon? _____

6. Ranch Dude Dan thinks the fencing competition is a bunch of cowboys putting up fences, and this he wants to see! How much will it cost for him and 7 ranch hands to go? _____

7. Which is a better price for the Achoo family of 2 kids and 2 adults: the fencing finals at 15% off, the swim events at 10% off, or 2-day track passes at 30% off? _____

8. Will Mr. Splash save more money if he gets 30% off both gymnastic events or 25% off the volleyball and golf tournaments? _____

9. The Lions Baseball League gets a 40% group discount. How much will they save when they buy tickets for 38 children and 20 adults to see the baseball game? _____

10. The tennis match and the volleyball game each have 5 seats left. If Ms. Courtside purchases them all at a 15% discount, how much money will the ticket center take in from her? _____

11. Mr. Cheapskate qualifies for the 15% miser's discount. Can he and his wife see both gymnastics events and the tennis match for under $100? _____

12. An old golf pro wants 22 tickets to the golf tournament. If he has a coupon for a 10% discount, can he get these tickets for under $700? _____

Name _____

35

THE VICTORY MEAL

The Panthers Basketball team is having a celebration meal after winning the big game against their rivals, the Coyotes. They're not thinking about it now, but the cost is adding up! Look at the bill for each player. Figure out how much each will spend by totaling the bill and adding a 6% tax and 15% tip. (Figure the tip on the food total only, not the total after tax is added.) What is the total bill for the team?

1. SARA

Nachos	4.00
Ham Sandwich	4.70
Choc. Shake	1.85

Subtotal _____

Tax _____

Tip _____

TOTAL _____

2. TARA

Egg Rolls	3.00
Rice Plate	3.50
Chow Mein	2.50
Iced Tea	1.00

Subtotal _____

Tax _____

Tip _____

TOTAL _____

3. KARA

Turkey Plate	6.00
Salad	3.25
Sundae	2.50

Subtotal _____

Tax _____

Tip _____

TOTAL _____

4. LARA

Pizza	7.00
Salad	3.25
Breadsticks	2.50
Cola	1.00

Subtotal _____

Tax _____

Tip _____

TOTAL _____

5. DARA

Cheese Sticks	1.65
Lasagna	6.50
Salad	3.25
Pie	1.50

Subtotal _____

Tax _____

Tip _____

TOTAL _____

6. COACH

Spaghetti	5.50
Garlic Bread	2.00
Salad	3.25
Iced Coffee	2.75

Subtotal _____

Tax _____

Tip _____

TOTAL _____

Name _____

7. TOTAL BILL = _____

DEEPWATER DEBT

Scuba Diver Scott bought all new equipment. He was not able to pay for it all at once, so he's making some monthly payments. The store is not charging interest. Fill in the blanks with the missing information about his payments.

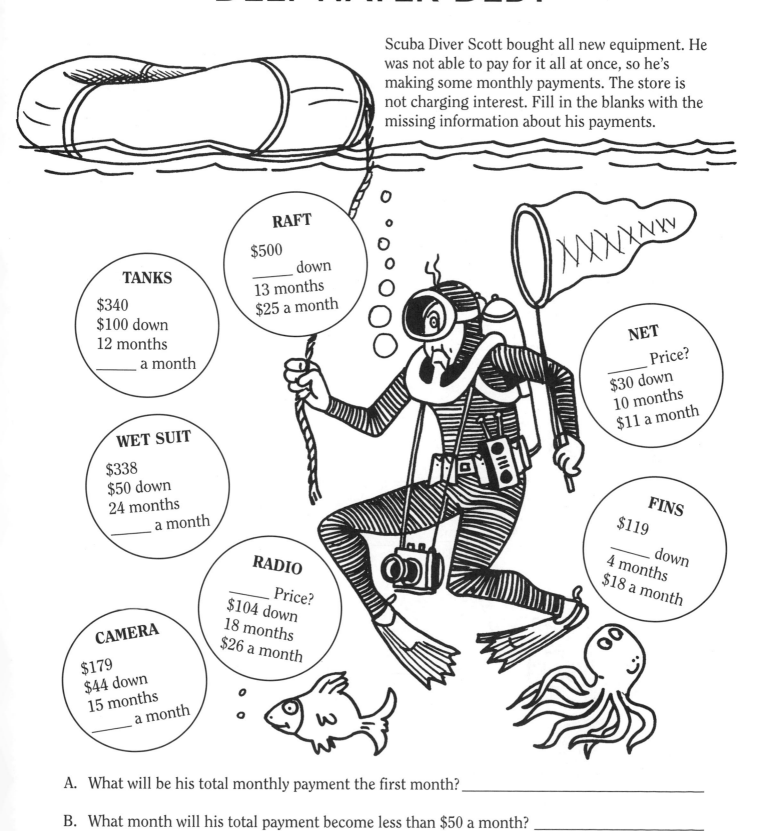

RAFT

$500

_____ down

13 months

$25 a month

TANKS

$340

$100 down

12 months

_____ a month

NET

_____ Price?

$30 down

10 months

$11 a month

WET SUIT

$338

$50 down

24 months

_____ a month

FINS

$119

_____ down

4 months

$18 a month

RADIO

_____ Price?

$104 down

18 months

$26 a month

CAMERA

$179

$44 down

15 months

_____ a month

A. What will be his total monthly payment the first month? _____

B. What month will his total payment become less than $50 a month? _____

Name _____

OUT OF GAS

The team has great batting averages, but Coach struck out at calculating his gas mileage for this trip. You can find out ahead of time what kind of mileage the van will get on their trips, or how much gas they'll need, by using these ratios:

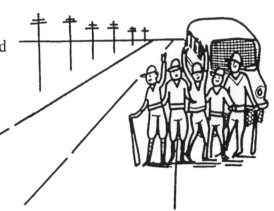

$$\frac{\text{miles}}{\text{gas used}} = \underline{\hspace{1cm}} \text{ miles per gallon (mpg)}$$

$$\frac{\text{miles}}{\text{miles per gallon (mpg)}} = \underline{\hspace{1cm}} \text{ gas used (in gallons)}$$

For questions 1-8, find the gas mileage (mpg). *(Round answers to the nearest tenth.)*

1. $\dfrac{400 \text{ mi}}{20 \text{ gal}} = \underline{\hspace{1cm}}$ mpg

2. $\dfrac{420 \text{ mi}}{25 \text{ gal}} = \underline{\hspace{1cm}}$ mpg

3. $\dfrac{252 \text{ mi}}{16.4 \text{ gal}} = \underline{\hspace{1cm}}$ mpg

4. $\dfrac{310 \text{ mi}}{21.6 \text{ gal}} = \underline{\hspace{1cm}}$ mpg

5. $\dfrac{199 \text{ mi}}{12.5 \text{ gal}} = \underline{\hspace{1cm}}$ mpg

6. $\dfrac{100.2 \text{ mi}}{12.6 \text{ gal}} = \underline{\hspace{1cm}}$ mpg

7. $\dfrac{515.8 \text{ mi}}{28.2 \text{ gal}} = \underline{\hspace{1cm}}$ mpg

8. $\dfrac{287.9 \text{ mi}}{17.3 \text{ gal}} = \underline{\hspace{1cm}}$ mpg

For questions 9-16, find the amount of gas used. *(Round answers to the nearest tenth.)*

9. $\dfrac{179 \text{ mi}}{10 \text{ mpg}} = \underline{\hspace{1cm}}$ gal

10. $\dfrac{226 \text{ mi}}{18.5 \text{ mpg}} = \underline{\hspace{1cm}}$ gal

11. $\dfrac{216 \text{ mi}}{22 \text{ mpg}} = \underline{\hspace{1cm}}$ gal

12. $\dfrac{344 \text{ mi}}{20.2 \text{ mpg}} = \underline{\hspace{1cm}}$ gal

13. $\dfrac{395 \text{ mi}}{23.1 \text{ mpg}} = \underline{\hspace{1cm}}$ gal

14. $\dfrac{133 \text{ mi}}{6 \text{ mpg}} = \underline{\hspace{1cm}}$ gal

15. $\dfrac{198 \text{ mi}}{12 \text{ mpg}} = \underline{\hspace{1cm}}$ gal

16. $\dfrac{395 \text{ mi}}{25 \text{ mpg}} = \underline{\hspace{1cm}}$ gal

JUST KEEP ON TRUCKIN'!..

COACH

GAS

NEXT GAS 8 mi

Name

WHITE WATER CALCULATIONS

To find the rate at which Katarina Kayaker paddles on her practice sessions on different runs, use this ratio:

$$\text{rate in miles per hour (mph)} = \frac{\text{distance}}{\text{time}}$$

If you know the rate, but not the time, use this ratio:

$$\text{time} = \frac{\text{distance}}{\text{rate (mph)}}$$

Fill in the missing information on the chart. Round answers to the nearest tenth.

	NAME of RUN	Distance	Time	Rate (mph)
1.	Wallawalla River Run	4.8 mi	.4 hrs	_____ mph
2.	Ripping Rapids	7.21 mi	.7 hrs	_____ mph
3.	Pacific Ocean Edge	8.64 mi	1.1 hrs	_____ mph
4.	Danger Drop Gorge	19.04 mi	1.6 hrs	_____ mph
5.	Crazy Canyon Rapids	4.09 mi	.66 hrs	_____ mph
6.	Watch-out Whirlpool	14.59 mi	.9 hrs	_____ mph
7.	Lazy Current	12.25 mi	2.5 hrs	_____ mph
8.	Twenty Falls River	29 mi	2.9 hrs	_____ mph
9.	Broken Back Bend	7.44 mi	.8 hrs	_____ mph
10.	Last Chance Gorge	14.08 mi	1.6 hrs	_____ mph
11.	Eternity Run	24.84 mi	_____ hrs	6.9 mph
12.	Snake River Scourge	6.16 mi	_____ hrs	8.8 mph
13.	Never Never Rapids	8.33 mi	_____ hrs	11.1 mph
14.	Big Wave Gorge	10.92 mi	_____ hrs	9.1 mph
15.	Switchback River	19.92 mi	_____ hrs	8.3 mph

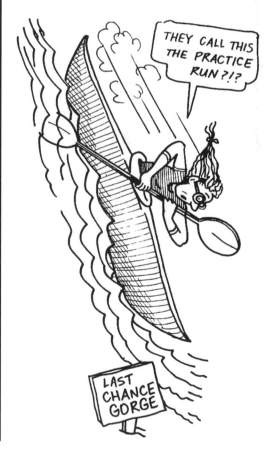

THEY CALL THIS THE PRACTICE RUN ?!?

LAST CHANCE GORGE

On what run does she have her fastest speed? _____

What run is the slowest? _____

Name _____

ON COURSE

At each of these courses, some information is missing. Find either the rate, time, or distance for each sport that has taken place there.

Remember that: distance (d) = rate (r) x time (t)

So: r = d/t and t = d/r

MOUNTAIN CLIMBER

1. mountain climber

13.5 mi

_____ hr

.5 mph

3. ski jumper

3 mi

_____ hr

60 mph

2. skier

_____ mi

3.33 hrs

7 mph

SKI JUMP

4. speed skater

300 meters

_____ min

75 meters per min

SPEED SKATE RINK

BOBSLED TRACK

MOUNTAIN BIKE RACE COURSE

6. bobsled racer

4.25 mi

.05 hr

_____ mph

5. powerboat pilot

_____ mi

.15 hr

120 mph

POWERBOAT RACES

8. race car driver

114 mi

.6 hr

_____ mph

7. mountain biker

35 mi

1.4 hr

_____ mph

RACE CAR TRACK

Name

INJURY PROBLEMS

Boxer Bruno has gotten injured 4 out of every 5 times he's had a match. If he's fought in 320 matches, how many times has he been injured?

You can answer this question by using this proportion: $4/5 = n/320$

Solve the proportion by cross multiplication:
5 times n = 4 times 320 (5 x n = 4 x 320 or 5n = 4 x 320).

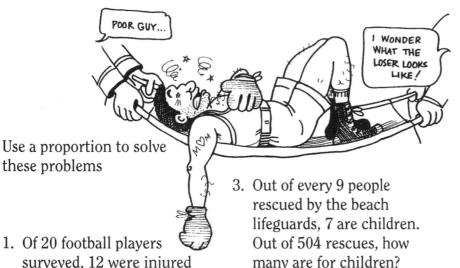

Use a proportion to solve these problems

1. Of 20 football players surveyed, 12 were injured last season. There are 80 players in the school football program. At this rate, how many injuries were there?

   _____

2. The cost of hospital visits for soccer team injuries averages $900 for the first 2 months of the season. At this rate, how much will injuries cost over the 5-month season?

   _____

3. Out of every 9 people rescued by the beach lifeguards, 7 are children. Out of 504 rescues, how many are for children?

   _____

4. Tennis player Tom lost 45 minutes over 3 games for a bloody nose. At this rate, how much time will be lost in 7 games?

   _____

5. Out of every 7 members on the ski team, 2 quit before the end of the season because of injuries. If 28 quit because of injuries, how many started the season?

   _____

6. The ratio of jumps to falls for ice skater Rhonda is 4 falls to every 15 jumps. At this rate, how many times will she NOT fall in 360 jumps?

   _____

7. 350 out of 500 bike injuries in the state last year were head injuries. Of each 10 bike injuries, how many are to the head?

   _____

8. The hurdlers on the Cougar team bang up their shins 35 times in 4 hours of practice. At this rate, how many shin injuries will there be in 300 hours of practice?

   _____

Name _____

IT'S ABOUT TIME

A volleyball team from Minneapolis is on the road for several weeks. They're on a tight schedule, so they have to pay attention to their time. Solve their time problems for them. Remember to consider time zone changes in your calculations.

1. Leave Minneapolis (CT) for Portland, Maine, (ET) at noon on Sunday. Arrive at 1 P.M. on Monday. How long did they travel?

   _____

2. Head out of Portland (ET) for Buffalo (ET) Monday at 7:30 P.M. for a 13-hour trip. Arrival time in Buffalo?

   _____ Time _____ Day

3. Drive 14 hours from Buffalo (ET) to Chicago (CT). Arrive at 5:15 A.M. on Friday. When did they leave Buffalo?

   _____ Time _____ Day

4. Travel from Chicago (CT), leaving after a party at midnight on Sunday. Arrive in Minneapolis (CT) for home game 8 hours later. Arrival time?

   _____ Time _____ Day

5. Leave Minneapolis (CT) for Salt Lake City (MT) at 6 A.M. Wednesday. Travel 38 hours plus a 5-hour delay for bad weather. Arrival time?

   _____ Time _____ Day

6. Fly from Salt Lake City (MT) to Calgary, Canada (MT). Plane leaves at 8:10 A.M. for a 1 hour 54 minute flight. Arrival time?

   _____

7. Fly from Calgary (MT) to Anchorage, Alaska (AT), on a 2 hour 20 minute flight leaving at 11:49 A.M. Arrival time?

   _____

8. Fly from Anchorage (AT) to meet bus in Seattle (PT). Flight departure, scheduled for 9:33 A.M. was delayed 1 hour 45 minutes. Flight is 2 hours 10 minutes long. Arrival time in Seattle?

   _____

9. Drive from Seattle (PT) to Denver (MT). Arrive 6:05 P.M. Monday in Denver after a 22 hour 30 minute trip. When did they leave Seattle?

   _____ Time _____ Day

10. Head home to Minneapolis (CT) from Denver (MT), leaving at 10:30 A.M. on Monday. Two 10-hour stops to sleep and eleven 30-minute stops for gas and food. The actual driving time is 26 hours. Arrival time home?

   _____ Time _____ Day

Name _____

42

DROP-IN SOLUTIONS

Some problems are open-ended problems. They have more than one possible answer. Solve these open-ended problems about sports.

1. Find two different numbers that could show how many jumps the skydiving team took today. The number is a 2-digit odd number under 40. Both digits are odd. The sum of the digits is 10; their product is odd. Tell at least two different numbers of jumps the team could have made.

_____

2. While golfer Greg was searching for his ball, he found 24 coins totaling $2.40. Tell two different combinations of coins he might have found.

_____

_____

3. At the end of a good game, three bowlers each had scores above 250 and the fourth had a score of 225. The total of all 4 scores was 1110, and no bowler scored a perfect 300. Name two possible combinations of the bowlers' scores.

_____

_____

4. There are 5 ways a football team can score points:
   6 pts......(TD) Touchdown
   3 pts......(FG) Field Goal
   2 pts......(R) Run after a touchdown
   1 pts......(K) Kick after a touchdown
   2 pts......(S) Safety
   Show 4 different ways a team could score 21 points in a game.

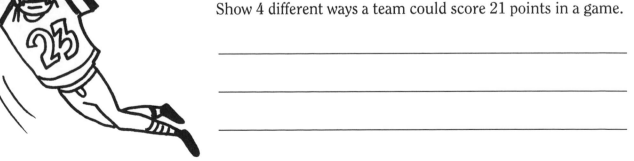

_____

_____

_____

_____

Name _____

SPEED DOESN'T COUNT

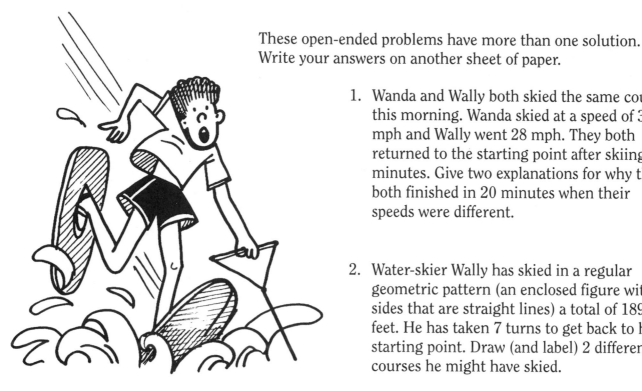

These open-ended problems have more than one solution. Write your answers on another sheet of paper.

1. Wanda and Wally both skied the same course this morning. Wanda skied at a speed of 35 mph and Wally went 28 mph. They both returned to the starting point after skiing 20 minutes. Give two explanations for why they both finished in 20 minutes when their speeds were different.

2. Water-skier Wally has skied in a regular geometric pattern (an enclosed figure with sides that are straight lines) a total of 1890 feet. He has taken 7 turns to get back to his starting point. Draw (and label) 2 different courses he might have skied.

3. Last week, skier Wally fell once more than half as much as Dan, who fell 3 times as often as Jen. Jen fell a number of times that has 2 even digits and is < 30. How many times did Wally fall? Give at least 2 different answers.

4. The gasoline tank on Dana's boat holds 26 gallons. Dana filled it up by carrying gas to her boat in a 3-gallon can and a 2-gallon can. Tell 3 different ways she could have filled her tank using these 2 cans to carry gas.

5. Ari, like all skiers, does a lot of bouncing across waves. Yesterday, he bounced a record number! The number of bounces is a 3-digit palindrome whose digits add up to 17. (A palindrome is a number that reads the same forwards and backwards.) All digits are < 7. How many times did Ari bounce? Give at least two possible answers.

Name

44

HORSING AROUND

For each problem, choose the problem-solving strategy that you think would be the best one to help you with the solution.

1. A jockey is 62 inches tall. Is this about 5 feet tall?

   a) Use mental math
   b) Draw a diagram
   c) Translate problem into a ratio

2. Each bale of hay in the barn is 2 cubic feet. The barn has 575 cubic feet of space. How many bales will fit in the barn?

   a) Use trial and error
   b) Make a number line
   c) Estimate

3. You know the times that 8 races begin and the lengths of each race. How will you set up a plan for 24 horses to race at different times?

   a) Translate into an equation
   b) Make a chart
   c) Use a formula

4. Horse C is ahead of Horse B who is 3 horses behind Horse F. Horse A is 2 horses ahead of Horse D, who is 2 horses ahead of Horse E. Which horse is closest to the finish line?

   a) Draw a diagram
   b) Use statistical data
   c) Use trial and error

5. Fresh Paint won 4 out of the last 13 races. At this rate, how many will he win in the next 65 races?

   a) Make a number line
   b) Estimate
   c) Translate into a proportion

6. You know the number of first place wins for 2 horses, Shooting Star and Record Breaker, for each of the past 10 years. You want to answer some questions about the comparison of their wins during these years.

   a) Write an equation
   b) Make a number line
   c) Make a graph

7. Heartbreaker runs for .15 hours and covers a distance of 4.95 miles. At what rate in miles per hour is he running?

   a) Translate into a ratio
   b) Trial and error
   c) Use mental math

8. 2500 spectators are seated in 6 stands. If 5 hold the same amount and the 6th holds 12 times that amount, how many spectators do the first 5 hold?

   a) Translate into a proportion
   b) Write an equation
   c) Estimate

Name _____

TO RIDE A WAVE

There are many strategies for solving problems. Sometimes one problem can be solved using more than one strategy. Choose a strategy that you think is best for each problem, and find the solution.

Trial and Error . . .
Write an Equation . . .
Make a Diagram . . .
Make a Chart . . .
Make a Graph . . .
Use Mental Math . . .
Estimate . . .
Use a Formula . . .
Make a Number Line . . .
Translate into a
Ratio or Proportion . . .
Guess and Check . . .

HEY, DUDE!

1. Hot Shot Surfer Stu catches 4 great waves every half hour. At this rate, how long will it be before he has ridden 44 waves?

   Answer _____

2. Beach Bum Bonnie is 75 feet from the shore at 9 A.M. Every hour she moves forward 18 feet and is pulled backward 7 feet. What time will she reach the shore?

   Answer _____

3. Two surfers, Al and Alison, have the same 2 digits in their ages, but the digits are reversed. $1/11$th of the sum of their ages is the square root of the differences between their ages plus 1. What are their ages?

   Answer _____

Name _____

HEAVY MATH FOR STRONG MINDS

The answer is given for each of these weighty problems. But is it correct? Check each answer for accuracy. Use any method you choose. For each problem write YES or NO to tell whether it is accurate. If it is incorrect, find the right answer.

HUH?

OX

1. Ox is 6 times the weight of Tiny, yet Tiny can lift Ox even when he's holding 80 pounds. Tiny is holding up 410 pounds right now (Ox plus 80 lbs). How much does Tiny weigh?
   55 lbs
   Accurate? _____

2. The number of bones in a weight lifter's foot is 26. How many bones are there in the feet of 26 weight lifters?
   676 bones
   Accurate? _____

3. Ox, Puduka's Weight Lifting Champion, added 28 pounds to each side of his bar. Then, he took off two 10-pound weights from each side and added seven 3-pound weights to each side. He began with 73 pounds on each side. How much TOTAL weight is there on the bar now?
   102 lbs
   Accurate? _____

4. Ox puts spherical weights at the ends of his bar. They have a radius of 5.5 inches. What is the volume of each weight? (The formula for the volume of a sphere is $\frac{4}{3}\pi r^3$.)
   696.6 in.³
   Accurate? _____

5. Ox eats 3.7 lbs of pasta every day for 10 days before a competition. How much pasta would he eat if he had 3 competitions this month?
   117 pounds
   Accurate? _____

6. The weight lifting team of 5 members ate 80 tacos in 12 minutes. On the average, how many tacos did each member eat per minute?
   1.3 tacos
   Accurate? _____

7. Ox lifted 203 pounds this morning. Zorro lifted 174 pounds. Write a ratio, in lowest terms, that compares Ox's lift to Zorro's.
   ⁶/₇
   Accurate? _____

8. At the end of every contest, Ox takes a walk around the mat 10 times. The mat is 30 x 40 feet. How far does he walk?
   1200 feet
   Accurate? _____

Name _____

YOUR FISH WAS HOW BIG?

Sometimes fishermen or fisherwomen (and other sports persons) stretch the truth about their accomplishments. For each of these sports tales, decide whether or not the answer is **reasonable.** If it is not, explain why.

YOU SHOULD HAVE SEEN THE ONE THAT GOT AWAY!

1. Fisherman Frank's fish weighed 2.2 pounds per foot. The scales showed a weight of 7.3 pounds. Frank claims his fish was 14.6 feet long. Is his claim reasonable?_____

2. Fisherman Frank is 40 years old. His son Frankie is 16. How many years ago was Frank 6 times as old as his son? Frankie calculates the answer to be 18 years. Is this reasonable?_____

3. Nicole's tennis balls have a radius of 1.25 inches. Her container for balls is a can 2.75 inches in diameter and 13 inches tall. She says her can holds 5 tennis balls. Is this reasonable? _____

4. Trixie the trampolinist bounces at a rate of 2 bounces every 6 seconds. At this rate, how long will it take her to bounce 3600 times? Trixie's answer is 20 minutes. Is this reasonable? _____

5. Brady bicyclist takes a ride one day at 25.4 mph for 8 hours. Wayne Walker takes a walk for the same amount of time at 3.5 mph. How many miles does each cover? Brady says he rides 203.2 miles and Wayne claims he walks 28 miles. Is this reasonable? _____

6. A volleyball tournament has 16 teams. A team is eliminated when they lose one game. Winners go on to play winners of other games. If 400 tickets are sold to each game, how many tickets will be sold for the tournament? Referee Rachael says 1000 tickets will be sold. Is this reasonable? _____

7. Pole-vaulter Paula leaps 2.1 times as far as her little sister Polly. Polly's highest leap is 5.8 feet. Paula claims her highest is 28 feet. Is this reasonable? _____

8. Cross-country skier Cassie skied at a pace of 3.8 mph for 4 hours and 6.3 mph for 22 hours one afternoon. She claims she skied a distance of 314.5 miles. Is this reasonable? _____

Name

APPENDIX

CONTENTS

PROBLEM-SOLVING STRATEGIES

One of the keys to successful problem solving is finding a strategy that works for that problem. If you get good at these strategies, you'll probably be able to tackle just about any problem you come across!

ESTIMATE

Many times you can figure out a solution by doing a rough or approximate calculation. This works well when you don't have to get a **precise** answer.

Maintenance workers want to set up several boxing rings in a huge sports center. They need a space 32 feet by 32 feet for each boxing ring area. The sports center is 300 feet x 280 feet. Can they set up 15 rings?

Round 32 to 30. They need about (30 x 30) 900 ft² for each ring. Then . . . round 280 to 300. The center is about (300 x 300) 90,000 ft². You can estimate that the center has room for about 10 rings, not 15. Then your solution is NO, they can't!

TRANSLATE INTO AN EQUATION

In many problems, you have a mixture of numbers and words. It is helpful to change the whole thing into a number sentence.

The rock-climbing team climbed 200 feet on Saturday, 35 feet less on Sunday, and 41 feet more on Monday than on Sunday. How far did they climb all together?

This can be changed into an equation:
x = 200 + (200 – 35) + (200 – 35 + 41)

GUESS AND CHECK

Sometimes the best strategy is to make a smart guess and then count or calculate to see if you are right. When you enter a contest to see who can come closest to the correct number of jelly beans in a jar, you are using this strategy.

HOW MANY JELLY-BEANS?

TRANSLATE INTO A PROPORTION

When the problem gives you a ratio and asks for a solution at the same rate, set up a proportion that will help you find the answer.

3 out of 16 skiers in the Himalayas claim to have seen the Abominable Snowman. At this rate, how many skiers out of 176 are likely to have seen the snowman?

Set up this proportion: $^3/_{16} = {}^x/_{176}$

MENTAL MATH

Solve simple problems in your head. Often you don't need pencil and paper or any other strategy!

To decide what time it will be in 3 hours 20 minutes, mentally count 3 hours ahead from 2 P.M. and 20 minutes ahead from 37 (to 2:57 P.M.).

TRIAL AND ERROR

For some problems, you just have to try out different solutions until you find one that works. Try out 2-digit even numbers until you find the answer to this problem:

The number of fans on the Booster Club bus is an even, 2-digit number. The sum of the digits is >10, the difference is < 5, and the product is < 34.

USE A FORMULA

When you need to find a measurement, such as for area or volume, make sure you look up the accurate formula. To find the area of this circle, use the formula $A = \pi r^2$ to find that the area is 113 ft².

6"

DRAW A GRAPH, CHART, OR TABLE

Sometimes it helps to create a quick graph, chart, or table to find solutions. This works best when you have statistical data that falls into different categories. For instance, if you need to answer questions about scores in 4 different quarters of a basketball game, it may help to put them on a table to get all the information in front of your eyes at once. This table can help you answer such questions as:

Which team benefited the most from foul shots in the first 3 quarters?

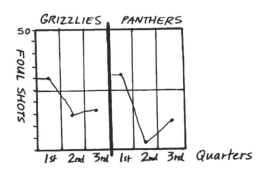

DRAW A DIAGRAM OR PICTURE

Some problems are just too complex to picture in your mind, so you need to sketch them out. A diagram will help you with this problem.

A hurdler, gymnast, equestrian, archer, and diver have just lined up to buy lunch. The diver is the 2nd person behind the archer. The hurdler is ahead of the equestrian. There are 3 people between the equestrian and archer.

Which one is at the end of the line?

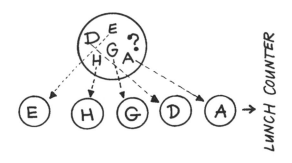

MAKE A MODEL

Create a model from paper, straws, blocks, or other materials if you need to visualize the problem to find a solution.

If you build a space figure with 8 faces, how many vertices (corners) will it have?

It will be easier to answer this question if you build a model out of straws and count the vertices.

MAKE A NUMBER LINE

If you are adding and/or subtracting a number of facts, it might be useful to draw a number line to help with your solution. Draw arrows for each step of the problem.

Evan walks 1.5 miles on Monday, 2 miles on Tuesday, 2 miles on Wednesday, .5 miles on Thursday, and 3.5 miles on Friday. How far has he walked this week?

```
0  1  2  3  4  5  6  7  8  9  10
|__|__|__|__|__|__|__|__|__|__|  MILES
```

USE LOGIC

Lots of math problems need a heavy dose of reasoning, or logic, to find a solution. This is often combined with other strategies. Often, using logic involves "If . . . Then" thinking, where you say to yourself, "If this is true, then this must be true." You can use logic in this kind of problem:

Julie has done more dives than Dylan. Dylan has done more dives than Andrea or Thomas. Who has done more dives, Andrea or Julie?
If $J > D$ and $D > A$, then $J > A$.

WORK BACKWARDS

Often it is helpful to start at the end of a problem and work backwards to find a missing fact.

Zak took a taxi home from the volleyball game. He gave the taxi driver $9.30, which included a $2.00 tip. The cab rate is $4.50 for the first 3 miles plus .20 a mile after that. How many miles was it from the gym to Zak's home?

$ 9.30 – $ 2.00 – $ 4.50 = $ 2.80
$ 2.80 ÷ 20 = 14 miles
14 miles + 3 miles = 17 miles

Subtract the $2.00 tip. Next subtract the amount for the first 3 miles. Then divide the remainder by .25. Take that amount and add the first 3 miles back on.

SIMPLIFY THE PROBLEM

Sometimes a problem can be made simpler by rewording it into a shorter or more straightforward question.

The coach makes the players run sprints for 15% of each practice. Practices are 2 hours long. How many minutes do they sprint?

Here's the problem stated in simpler terms: What is 15% of 2 hours?

CHANGE FACTS TO A COMMON ELEMENT

When you have facts that include different units, change the mixture into a common element, usually the smallest unit. Change yards and feet into inches. Change hours into minutes. For this problem, change gallons and quarts into pints.

The team drank ½ gallon of sports drink. Jan drank 2 quarts, Samantha drank 3 pints, Amy drank 7 pints, and Drew drank 1 quart. How much did the rest of the team drink?

1 gal = 8 pints so 12 gal = 96 pints
1 qt = 4 pints so 2 qt = 8 pints
96 – 8 – 7 – 4 = 77 pints

WEED OUT UNNECESSARY INFORMATION

Some problems have information you do not need. This excess information just complicates the problem, so it's good to be able to sort out what is **not** needed in order to find a solution.

Jenna's horse refused 4 jumps today, and cleared 12. Yesterday, the horse cleared 7 jumps more than today. She won 2 first place ribbons. How many jumps did the horse clear in the 2-day jumping event?

The information that is **not** needed is: the 4 jumps refused and the 2 first place ribbons.

LOOK FOR A PATTERN

Many problems involve an orderly arrangement of things or facts. Discovering the pattern can help you answer questions and find solutions. Look for the pattern in math problems!

Carmen's race times in her first 7 races were (in minutes): 5:25, 5:21, 4:17, 4:13, 4:09, 4:05, 4:01. Haley's times were 6:00, 5:78, 5:56, 5:34, 5:12, 4:90, 4:78. What will each girl's next 3 race times probably be?

If you look for a pattern, you will see that Carmen has shaved .04 minutes off each race and Haley has shortened each by .12 minutes. Once you know the pattern, you can answer the question.

RECOGNIZE UNSOLVABLE PROBLEMS

If a problem doesn't have enough information, then you just can't solve it. When you begin working on a problem, first look to see what it tells you. Decide if there is enough information there to work toward a solution. The following problem is an example of one that is not solvable.

The hockey team traveled on a bus in the snowstorm for 47 hours 13 minutes after they left their hometown of Ontario. They had six delays and stops of 14 hours each. What time did they arrive in Denver?

52

GLOSSARY

ALGORITHM .... A formula commonly used for performing computations involving mathematical operations.

AVERAGE .... The sum of a set of numbers divided by the number of addends.
The average of 1, 2, 7, 3, 8, and 9 $= \dfrac{1 + 2 + 7 + 3 + 8 + 9}{6} = 5.$

CHANCE .... The probability or likelihood of an occurrence.

COMPOSITE NUMBER .... A number having at least one whole number factor other than 1 and itself.

CONSUMER PROBLEMS .... Math problems related to buying and selling and other financial events in the real world.

DATA .... A set of scores or information.

DIAGRAM .... A drawing used to illustrate a problem or problem solution.

DIGIT .... A symbol used to write numerals. The decimal system's digits are 0-9.

DISCOUNT .... A deduction made from the regular price of an item.

DIVISIBILITY .... A number is divisible by a given number if the quotient is a whole number.
189 is divisible by 9 because 21 (189 ÷ 9) is a whole number.

DOWN PAYMENT .... An amount of money, less than the whole purchase price of an item, given as an initial payment toward the whole purchase price.

EQUATION .... A mathematical sentence which states that two expressions are equal.
7 x 9 = 3 + (4 x 15) is an equation.

ESTIMATE .... An approximation or rough calculation.

ESTIMATION .... A process of giving an approximate answer to a problem.

EVEN NUMBER .... One of the set of whole numbers having 2 as a factor.

FACTOR .... One of 2 or more numbers that can be multiplied to find a product.
In the equation 7 x 6 = 42, 7 and 6 are factors of 42.
1, 2, 3, 14, and 21 are also factors of 42.

FREQUENCY .... The number of times a given item occurs in a set of data.

FREQUENCY GRAPH .... A way to organize and picture data using a grid.

FREQUENCY TABLE .... Data arranged on a table to show how often events occur.

FORMULA .... A rule or fact expressed in mathematical numbers and symbols.

GRAPH .... A drawing showing relationships between sets of numbers.

INEQUALITY .... A number sentence showing that two groups of numerals stand for
different numbers. The signs < and > show inequality.
4 + 9 < 7 + 10 is a statement of inequality.

INSTALLMENT PAYMENTS .... An amount of money paid on a regular basis toward the cost of
an item.

INTEREST .... A charge for borrowed money, usually a percentage of the amount
borrowed or owed.

INTERSECTION OF SETS .... The set of members common to each of two or more sets.

LOGIC .... A way of solving problems that involves using principles of reasoning.

MEAN .... Average: the sum of numbers in a set divided by the number
of addends.
The mean of 6, 8, 9, 19, 38 is 80 ÷ 5, or 16.

MENTAL MATH .... Solving problems in your head without using any tools.

MULTIPLE .... The product of a whole number and any other whole number.
12 is a multiple of 3 because 3 x 4 = 12.

MULTI-STEP PROBLEM .... A problem that requires more than one operation, process, or step in
order to reach a solution.

ODD NUMBER .... A whole number from the set of numbers equal to (n x 2) + 1.
1, 3, 5, 7, 9, . . . are odd numbers.

OPEN-ENDED PROBLEM .... A problem which has more than one solution.

OUTCOME .... A possible result in a probability experiment.

PALINDROME .... A number which reads the same forward and backward. *343 and 87678 are palindromes.*

PERCENT .... A comparison of a number with 100. *43 compared to 100 is 43%.*

PRIME NUMBER .... A number that has as its only whole number factors one and itself. *2, 3, 7, and 11 are examples of prime numbers.*

PROBABILITY .... The likelihood that an event will occur.

PROBLEM-SOLVING
STRATEGY .... A method of finding the solution to a problem.

PROPORTION .... A number statement of equality between two ratios. *Example: ³/₇ = ⁹/₂₁*

RATE .... A comparison of two quantities.

RATIO .... A comparison of two numbers expressed as ª/b, meaning a ÷ b.

ROUNDING .... Getting an approximate amount by dropping the digits after a given place and increasing the last digit by one if the first number that is dropped is 5 or larger.

SET .... A collection of items (called members or elements).

SOLUTION SET .... The set of possible solutions for a number sentence.

SOLUTION .... The number that replaces a variable to complete an equation.

SQUARE .... The result of a number being multiplied by itself. *144 is the square of 12 because 12 x 12 = 144.*

SQUARE ROOT .... A number, which when multiplied by itself, yields a given product. *The square root of 25 = 5 because 5 x 5 = 25.*

STATISTICS .... Numerical facts or data.

UNION OF SETS .... A set containing the combined members of two or more sets.

VARIABLE .... A symbol in a number sentence which could be replaced by a number. *In 3 + 9x = 903, x is the variable.*

PROBLEM-SOLVING
SKILLS TEST

All problems are worth 2 points each. For questions 1-12, write the letter of the correct answer.

Use the picture below to answer problems 1-3.

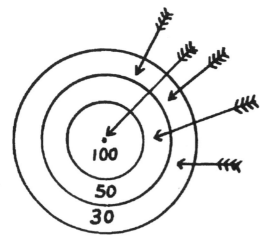

_____ 1. The total score received from these 5 arrows is
    a. over 250   c. under 200
    b. exactly 210   d. exactly 240

_____ 2. The ratio that shows the number of arrows scoring 30 to the number scoring over 30 is
    a. $\frac{3}{5}$ c. $\frac{2}{3}$
    b. $\frac{3}{2}$ d. $\frac{5}{3}$

_____ 3. If the next three arrows shot are 30, 30, and 100, what will be the average score for all the arrows shot?
    a. 50   c. 45
    b. 40   d. 80

_____ 4. Jana's pulse rate tripled during her morning run. Her resting pulse was 63. To find her pulse rate during her run, you should
    a. add
    b. multiply
    c. multiply, then add
    d. divide

_____ 5. Sports drinks cost 75 cents a bottle. Each player on the volleyball team drinks 3 a game. There are 17 players. To find how much the team spends on drinks over 4 games, you would
    a. multiply 4 times
    b. add, then multiply
    c. multiply twice
    d. multiply 3 times

_____ 6. A bowler knocked down an average of 6 pins in each frame. She bowled 30 frames every day for 10 days. A good problem-solving strategy for finding out how many pins she knocked down in 10 days would be
    a. make a number line
    b. use mental math
    c. translate into a ratio
    d. draw a diagram

_____ 7. 4 pole vaulters line up in order of their height. Bob is taller than Bill and Bud. Brad is shorter than Bob and Bill. Brad is taller than Bud. To find out who is tallest, a good problem–solving strategy would be
    a. make a graph
    b. estimate
    c. write an equation
    d. draw a diagram

_____ 8. 288 hot dogs were sold during the first 3 innings of the baseball game. 506 more were sold during innings 3–7. During the 7th inning stretch, they sold 390. Another 113 were sold during innings 8 and 9. A good estimate of the total sold would be
    a. 1000   c. 1300
    b. 1100   d. 1200

Name

_____ 9. Hockey Team A has scored twice as many goals as Team B, who has scored 6 goals. Team C has scored 3 less than A and B together. Which equation represents the number of goals Team C has scored?
   a. n = 2(6 + 3) − 3
   b. n = 6 + (6 x 2) − 3
   c. n = 6 − (3 x 2) + 6
   d. n = 2(6−3) + 6

_____ 10. Zoie sold her wet suit to a friend for $146 and her snorkel and mask for $95 less. Then she bought a used suit for $90 and a used mask and snorkel for $26. Which equation shows how much money she still has?
   a. n = 146 − 95 + 90 − 26
   b. n = 90 + 26 − 146 − 95
   c. n = 146 + 95 − 90 − 26
   d. n = 146 + (146 − 95) − 90 − 26

_____ 11. Dr. Foil gave 16 physical exams to the fencing team members. Dr. Goal gave 3 less than twice as many to the soccer team. Which equation represents the number Dr. Goal gave?
   a. n = (2 x 16) − 3
   b. n = (2 x 16) / 3
   c. n = 16 + (3 x 2) − 3
   d. n = 16 − 3/2

_____ 12. Chen Li had 3 more than twice as many injuries as Amy. Together the 2 had 18. Which equation shows this situation?
   a. x + 2x − 3 = 18
   b. x + 3/2 = 18
   c. x + (2x + 3) = 18
   d. 2x + 3 − x = 18

For questions 13–50, write the correct answer on the line.

_____ 13. Estimate the answer to this problem: Hockey practice lasted 4 hours each day last week except for Friday and Saturday. On these days the team practiced 6 hours 45 minutes. There is no practice on Sunday. What was the average length of a practice?

_____ 14. 1658 football fans attended Friday's game. 152 left before half time. 823 sat in reserved seats. 82 fans left during halftime. 221 left during the 3rd and 4th quarters. What information is NOT needed to find out how many fans were left at the end of the game?

_____ 15. Tickets to the swim meet cost $8.50 for adults, $3.00 for children, $6.00 for senior citizens, and $ 5.00 for students. The total receipts for the game were $9670.00. What **missing** information do you need in order to find out how many students were at the game?

_____ 16. Carla does 161 pushups a week. She does 14 on Monday and 27 on Tuesday. What **missing** information do you need to find out the percent of the total she has finished by Thursday?

_____ 17. James scored 16 runs in 4 baseball games. He scored 4 in Game 1 and 3 less than twice as many in Game 2. He had 5 hits in Game 3 and scored 4 in Game 4. Which information is NOT needed to find out how many runs he scored in Game 2?

_____ 18. Natasha knocked down 2 out of 9 hurdles. At this rate, she figures she will knock down 24 out of the next 108. Is this accurate?

_____ 19. Springs on Yuri's trampoline cost $2.59 each, and he estimates that he can replace all 98 of them for under $250.00. Is he correct?

Name

_____ 20. A golfer hit a ball at 10:59 A.M. Eastern Standard Time across a state line into the Central Standard Time Zone. The ball was in the air for over 1 minute. He claims that it landed in the next time zone at 12:01 P.M. Central Standard Time. Is he correct?

_____ 21. Find two different solutions for the following problem: The number of dives James took today is a 2-digit prime number. The sum of the digits are = or < 10, and the difference is equal to or greater than 4. What number is it?

_____ 22. Find two different solutions for the following problem: Ty and Cy both slept more than 6 hours a night the 3 nights before the ski race. Ty slept a total of 8 hours more than Cy. Neither slept a total of more than 33 hours. How many hours did Ty sleep each night? (He slept the exact same number each night.)

CONFERENCE 2-YEAR WIN-LOSS RECORD			
	Wins	Losses	Ties
Panthers	4	16	0
Grizzlies	20	0	0
Rams	15	3	2
Cougars	1	19	0
Kings	8	12	0
Cyclones	10	8	2

Use this table to solve problems 23–26.

23. What team had the second best win–loss record? _____

24. How many teams had a worse record than the Kings? _____

25. What was the total number of games played by the Cougars in the 2-year period? _____

26. How many games did the Cyclones **not** win over the 2-year period? _____

27. Brie exercises her horse by running him around a ring which has a radius of 11 feet. If the horse completes this circle 127 times, how far does he run? _____

28. Two friends need 50 square feet of blanket to wrap them up and keep them warm at a football game. They have a blanket that is 5 feet long and 4½ feet wide. Is it big enough? _____

Use this graph to solve problems 29-31.

SKI TEAM TRYOUTS

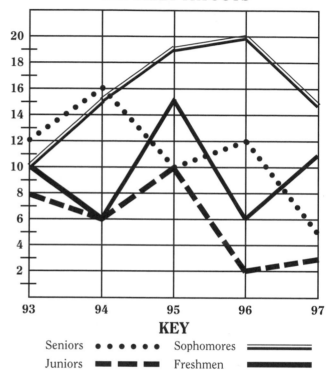

KEY

Seniors • • • • •   Sophomores ═══════

Juniors ▬ ▬ ▬ ▬   Freshmen ▬▬▬▬

29. Which class has the greatest increase in tryouts over a 2-year period? _____

30. Which classes had the same number of tryouts in 1995? _____

31. Which class has consistently had the lowest number of tryouts over the 5-year period? _____

32. Surfer Samantha has caught a ride on 3 out of the last 32 waves. At this rate, how many rides will she get out of the next 192 waves? _____

33. The Coast Tennis Training Camp accepts 4 out of 7 kids who apply. If 56 are accepted, how many applied? _____

Name

34. In a motorcycle race, Jed drives 242 miles in 2.75 hours. What is his speed? _____

35. Paula's powerboat goes 283.5 miles on 5 gallons. What kind of mileage is she getting? _____

36. Sue's soccer game ran long because of an overtime and a shoot-out. The game started at 1:45 P.M. and ended at 4:03 P.M. How long did the game last? _____

37. Thomas is catching up on his sleep after a tournament in Europe. He wakes at 6:30 A.M. on Thursday. He went to sleep at 11:11 P.M. on Tuesday. How long ago was that? _____

38. Marta has 7 hours and 13 minutes left to practice and rest before she takes her skating test. It is now 8:55 A.M. What time is her test? _____

39. 3 skateboarders are ages 12, 14, and 17. One has a brand-new board, one has an old beat-up board, and one uses a borrowed board. Jody is not 17. The owner of the old board is younger than Jen. Jo is older than Jody. The 12-year-old has the new board. The old board owner is not 17. Which skater has the used board? _____

40. 4 basketball teams compare the heights of their players. The Tigers are taller than the Panthers. The Vikings are shorter than the Chargers and the Tigers. The Panthers are shorter than the Vikings. The Tigers are taller than the Chargers. Which team has the tallest players? _____

41. Jan bought 3 videotapes of the surfing contest. They cost $16 each, plus 8% tax. How much did she pay? _____

42. Ski calendars that are regularly priced at $18 are on sale for 25% off. How much would Tori pay for 7 calendars? _____

43. Team A ate 12% less pasta than Team B. Team B ate 22 pounds. How much did Team A eat? _____

44. 40% of all the first-time sky divers who take lessons at the Take-a-Leap Sky Diving School get cold feet and don't jump. They had 510 first-time students last year. At this rate, how many jumped? _____

45. Attendance at the second district track meet was 1,925. The first meet's attendance was 76% of that. How many attended the first meet? _____

46. 730 fans came to see the Blue Ridge County Equestrian competition. 20% of them traveled about 100 miles to get there. 60% of them only traveled about 5 miles. The rest traveled about 30 miles. About how many miles did all the fans travel? _____

47. The wrestling team uses 12 bars of soap each time they shower. They have had 6 practices and 2 meets a week this season. They shower after each of these. How many bars of soap has the team used in a 13-week season? _____

48. Heptathlon Camp for junior athletes began on Wednesday, August 21, at noon. It ended 143 hours later. When was that? (Day, date, time?) _____

49. Anika paid $860 for gold-coated skates. They last for about 125 days of skating. She skates 6 days a week. How much will skates cost her a year? _____

50. The cross-country ski team burns up 228,000 calories in 3 races. There are 20 team members. Assuming each person burns the same amount in each race, how many calories does each member burn in each race? _____

SCORE: Total Points _____ out of a possible 100 points

Name _____

PROBLEM SOLVING
SKILLS TEST ANSWER KEY

Give 2 points to each correct answer. Total possible score is 100 points.

1. d
2. b
3. a
4. b
5. d
6. b
7. d
8. c
9. b
10. d
11. a
12. c
13. about 5 hours
14. 823 sat in reserved seats
15. the number of adults, children, and senior citizens who attended
16. the number of pushups Carla did on Wednesday and Thursday
17. 5 hits in Game 3 and the score of 4 runs in Game 4
18. yes
19. no
20. no
21. Give 1 point each for any two of these answers: 17, 19, 37, 61, 71, 73, 91
22. Give 1 point each for any two answers which are greater than 6 hours and equal to or less than 8.33 hours.
23. Rams

24. 2
25. 20
26. 10
27. 8773.16 feet
28. no
29. sophomore class
30. junior and senior classes
31. junior class
32. 18 rides
33. 98 applied
34. 88 miles per hour (mph)
35. 56.7 miles per gallon (mpg)
36. 2 hours 18 minutes
37. 31 hours 19 minutes
38. 4:08 P.M.
39. Jen
40. Tigers
41. $51.84
42. $94.50
43. 19.36 pounds
44. 306 jumped (204 did not)
45. 1463 attended
46. 21,170 miles
47. 1248 bars of soap
48. Tuesday, August 27, at 11:00 A.M.
49. $2580.00 spent in a year
50. 3800 calories per person per race

ANSWERS

Pages 10-11
1. a .... Answer: 20 races
2. a, b .... Answer: $264
3. a, b, c .... Answer: 21 hrs, 50 min
4. b, d .... Answer: 16/52 (or 4/13 in lowest terms)
5. a, b, c .... Answer: Week 5
6. b, c .... Answer: 3111 calories
7. a, c .... Answer: 600 fans
8. b, c .... Answer: 40%
9. d, e .... Answer: 16.4 meters
10. a, b, c .... Answer: 889, 600 ft²

Page 12
1. the number of his medals
   the number of competitor's medals
2. the depth of the pool
3. the number of times she practices each dive
4. the total number of towels
5. Maria's highest dive
6. the score of the 6th judge
7. the depth of the pool
8. dates of the titles
   or the number earned at the '84 Olympics and after
9. the team average

Page 13
1. • left home at 11 A.M.
   • returned at 2:30 P.M.
   • pulse was 145 bpm
   Answer: 4.57 mph

2. • left home at 9:18 A.M.
   • ran 2.6 miles to Sam's
   Answer: 5.8 miles

3. • 6 vegetarian
   • 4 plain
   • 2 pepperoni
   Answer: 12/18 or 2/3

4. • best time for 10 k 55 minutes
   • ran .16 k per minute
   Answer: 1 hr 4 min

5. • winner was 36 years old
   • average age was 28
   Answer: 285

6. • spent $60
   Answer: $840

7. • went to 12 meets
   • spent $490
   Answer: 719 miles

8. • uniforms cost $55
   Answer: 216 pieces

Page 14
1. 0	7. 22	13. 10
2. 39	8. 26	14. 7
3. 20	9. 2	15. 30
4. 4	10. 0	16. 40
5. 1	11. 22	17. 0
6. 2	12. 0	18. 0

Page 15
1. multiply
   Answer: $1800
2. multiply, add
   Answer: Tropic Jet, $885
3. multiply, add, subtract
   Answer: $40
4. multiply
   Answer: no
5. multiply, add
   Answer: Jamaica on Paradise Air
6. multiply, add
   Answer: Bermuda on Tropic Jet

Page 16
1. $7.12
2. Mon-Fri, 8 A.M.-5 P.M.
3. $10.90
4. $5.53
5. $44.18, more
6. 15 minutes
7. girlfriend
8. $ 19.57
9. 43 minutes
10. 21 minutes

Page 18
1. Queenie
2. 13
3. Queenie
4. Sophia
5. Queenie
6. 95
7. 90-91-92
8. Sophia
9. 1992
10. Sophia
11. 1994
12. Sophia

Page 19
1. Wagon Wheel Rodeo
   Batty Baseball Field
2. 1000
3. Basketville Basketball Gym
4. 12,000
5. about 6500
6. 7000
7. Dragtona Dog Race Track & Topnotch Tennis Courts
8. about 12,000

Page 20
1. Salt Lake City
2. about 700 miles
3. about 1500 miles
4. I-40 W to Knoxville and I-81 N to New York, about 1100 miles
5. San Antonio, Phoenix, or Oklahoma City
6. about 1200 miles
7. Boston
8. no, I-90 E to I-25, I-25 S to I-40 and I-40 E to Oklahoma City

Page 21
1. 19
2. 82
3. 19/82
4. 30.8%
5. Game 8
6. Games 5 and 8
7. 63
8. Games 1, 2, 3
9. 14
10. 112
11. 14/112 or 1/8
12. 71
13. 89%
14. 16
15. Games 1, 5, 7
16. Game 3

Page 22
1. 188.4 ft
2. 1230 ft
3. 1404 ft²
4. 1140 ft
5. 256 ft²
6. 87.9 ft
7. 153.9 ft²
8. 6672 ft²
9. 360 ft
10. 216 ft²

Page 23

1. 450
2. 232
3. 165
4. 2/19
5. 1 hr, 26 min (or 86 min)
6. 75 beats per min
7. 310 min
8. $ 24.00
9. 11
10. 4 times
11. 44 meters
12. 32 back stretches
13. Friday
14. 42 minutes

Page 24

Answers will be approximate. Give credit for anything close to amount below.

Sam Surf	$ 5.00
Hot-Shot Sally	$ 5.50
Dare Devil Darla	$ 5.50
Fearless Fred	$ 5.00
Mad Dog Maria	$ 9.00
Cool Cal	$ 4.00
Jack Snack	$ 7.00
No Way Jose	$ 8.50
Big Wave Will	$ 5.00
Beach Bum Bea	$ 5.00
Speedo Sara	$ 8.00
Never-Lose Ned	$ 5.50
Refill Ron	$ 5.00

Page 25

1. Equation: a Solution: 72 times
2. Equation: c Solution: 27¼ hrs
3. Equation: b Solution: 18 members
4. Equation: b Solution: 3.3 min.
5. Equation: a Solution: 15 medals
6. Equation: b Solution: 22

Page 26

Equations students write may differ slightly from these answers, but must include the same elements.

1. $n = 17{,}964 - 880 - 1000$
   Answer: 16,084

2. $n = 3(44) - 8$
   Answer: 124

3. $26 = 4n - 6$
   Answer: 8

4. $n = 42(12) - 12$
   Answer: 492

5. $n = 12.00 - 4(.75) - 3(1.00) + 6(.25) - 3.45$
   Answer: $ 4.05

6. $n = \dfrac{1087 - 34}{13}$
   Answer: 81

Page 27

Day 1	32
Day 2	6
Day 3	7
Day 4	33
Day 5	15
Day 6	64
Day 7	30
Day 8	9
Day 9	12
Day 10	111

Page 28

1. Day 37
2. 15
3. Yes
4. Day 20

Page 29

1. Tom poodle 16
   Order: Tara iguana 14, Tish llama 15, Tom poodle 16, Tori tarantula 17, Tad pig 18
2. #3 QB Tyler
   Order: #8 Guard Elijah, #3 QB Tyler, #4 Tackle Sean, #17 Fullback Ray, #2 Center Craig

Page 30

Answers in bold print.
1. **Kai**, Raoul, Hank, Guy, Jake, Daryl
2. **Anya**, Carla, Meghan, Fran, Patrice, Tonia
3. Gabe, Josh, **Wynn,** Andy, Bryan
4. Tami, Trina, Tracy, Trish, **Tori**

Page 31

1. 3 quarters, 6 dimes, 2 pennies
2. 5 quarters, 8 dimes, 1 nickel or 7 quarters and 7 nickels
3. 32 kids
4. 49 trampolinists
5. 15 steps

Page 32

1. 18%
2. 9%
3. 22 shots
4. 49 days
5. 58%
6. 27.5%
7. $ 51.00
8. 15 members
9. 20%
10. 135 shots

Page 33

1. $ 243.45, $ 48.69, $ 194.76
2. $ 126.70, $ 63.35, $ 63.35
3. $ 322.35, $96.71, $ 225.64
4. $ 233.94, $23.39, $ 210.55
5. $ 73.95, $ 11.09, $ 62.86
6. $ 243.23

Pages 34-35

1. $ 190.40
2. $ 111.00
3. $ 52.00
4. $ 343.20
5. $ 180.00
6. $ 288.00
7. swim events
8. volleyball and golf
9. $ 505.60
10. $ 238.00
11. yes
12. no

Page 36

1.	Sara	$ 12.76
2.	Tara	$ 12.10
3.	Kara	$ 14.22
4.	Lara	$ 16.64
5.	Dara	$ 15.61
6.	Coach	$ 16.34
7.	Total	$ 87.67

Page 37

Raft	$ 175 down
Tanks	$ 20 a month
Wet Suit	$ 12 a month
Radio	$ 572 price
Camera	$ 9 a month
Net	$ 140 price
Fins	$ 47 down

A. $ 121.00 a month
B. month 14

Page 38

1. 20 mpg
2. 16.8 mpg
3. 15.4 mpg
4. 14.4 mpg
5. 15.9 mpg
6. 8 mpg
7. 18.3 mpg
8. 16.6 mpg
9. 17.9 gal
10. 12.2 gal
11. 9.8 gal
12. 17 gal
13. 17.1 gal
14. 22.2 gal
15. 16.5 gal
16. 15.8 gal

Page 39

1. 12 mph
2. 10.3 mph
3. 7.9 mph
4. 11.9 mph
5. 6.2 mph
6. 16.2 mph
7. 4.9 mph
8. 10 mph
9. 9.3 mph
10. 8.8 mph
11. 3.6 hrs
12. .7 hrs
13. .75 hrs
14. 1.2 hrs
15. 2.4 hrs

Fastest: Watchout Whirlpool
Slowest: Lazy Current

Page 40

1. 27 hours
2. 23.31 miles
3. .05 hours
4. 4 minutes
5. 18 miles
6. 85 mph
7. 25 mph
8. 190 mph

page 41

1. 48
2. $ 2250
3. 392
4. 105 minutes (or 1 hr, 45 min)
5. 98
6. 264
7. 7
8. 2625

Page 42

1. 24 hours
2. 8:30 A.M. on Tuesday
3. 4:15 P.M. on Thursday
4. 8:00 A.M. on Monday
5. 12:00 A.M. on Friday
6. 10:04 A.M.
7. 12:09 P.M.
8. 2:28 P.M.
9. 7:35 P.M. on Sunday
10. 3:00 P.M. on Wednesday

Page 43

Answers will vary. Students are to give 2 answers for each problem. Give credit to students for any workable solution.

Page 44

Answers will vary. Students are to give 2 answers for each problem. Give credit to students for any workable solution.

Page 45

1. a
2. c
3. b
4. a
5. c
6. c
7. a
8. b

Page 46

Students should show that they have chosen and used a specific problem-solving strategy for each of these.
1. 5.5 hours
2. about 3-4 P.M.
3. ages 12 and 21
(other possible solutions)

Page 47

1. yes
2. no, There are 1352 bones in **2 feet** each of 26 persons
3. no, 204 pounds
4. yes
5. no, 111 pounds
6. yes
7. no, ⅛
8. no, 1400 feet

Page 48

Students will be explaining why they do not find answers reasonable. Accept any sensible explanation for their decisions.
1. no
2. no
3. yes
4. no
5. yes
6. no
7. no
8. no